NEIL LABUTE

The Shape of Things

Neil LaBute **The Shape of Things**

Herausgegeben von: Michael Thürwächter
Verlagsredaktion: Neil Porter
Umschlaggestaltung: Cornelsen Design
Umschlagfoto: (Statue) © Shutterstock / Curioso; (Pflaster) © Shutterstock / Misunseo
Layout und technische Umsetzung: Annika Preyhs für Buchgestaltung +, Berlin

www.cornelsen.de

1. Auflage, 6. Druck 2025

This edition is the complete and unabridged text of the play.

Alle Drucke dieser Auflage sind inhaltlich unverändert
und können im Unterricht nebeneinander verwendet werden.

© 2018 Cornelsen Verlag GmbH, Mecklenburgische Str. 53, 14197 Berlin,
E-Mail: service@cornelsen.de

Druck: AZ Druck und Datentechnik GmbH, Kempten

ISBN 978-3-06-036143-4

PEFC-zertifiziert
Dieses Produkt
stammt aus
nachhaltig
bewirtschafteten
Wäldern und
kontrollierten Quellen
PEFC/04-31-2260   www.pefc.de

Contents

Abbreviations and Annotations

adj	adjective		infml	informal
adv	adverb		n	noun
AE	American English		pl	plural
derog	derogatory		sb.	somebody
e.g.	exempli gratia; for example		sl	slang
esp.	especially		sth.	something
etc.	et cetera; and so on		usu.	usually
fml	formal		v	verb

The annotations are arranged chronologically; the first time a word is used is where you will find it explained.

The Shape of Things premiered in London at the Almeida Theatre on 24 May 2001 with the following cast:

Evelyn Rachel Weisz
Adam Paul Rudd
Jenny Gretchen Mol
Phillip Frederick Weller

Director Neil LaBute
Set Design Giles Cadle
Costume Design Lynette Meyer
Lighting Mark Henderson
Sound Fergus O'Hare
Casting Fiona Weir
Assistant Director David Salter

This production transferred to the Promenade Theatre, New York, opening on 10 October 2001, with the above cast and creative team.

CHARACTERS

Evelyn
Adam
Jenny
Phillip

Setting a liberal arts college in a conservative mid-western town
Author's note The / in certain lines denotes an attempt at inter-
    ruption or overlap by a given character

A MUSEUM

Silence. Darkness.

A young woman stands near a stretch of velvet rope.

She has a can in one hand and stares up at an enormous human sculpture. After a moment, a young man (in uniform) steps across the
5 *barrier and approaches her.*

Adam: ... You stepped over the line. Miss[1]? / Umm, you stepped over ...

Evelyn: I know. / It's 'ms[2]'.

Adam: Okay, sorry, ms, but, ahh ...

10 **Evelyn:** I meant to. / Step over ...

Adam: What? / Yeah, I figured you did. I mean, the way you did it and all, kinda deliberate like. / You're not supposed to do that.

Evelyn: I know. / That's why I tried it ...

Adam: Why?

15 **Evelyn:** ... To see what would happen.

Adam: Oh. Well ... Me, I s'pose[3].

Evelyn: 'Me'?

Adam: No, I mean, I'm what happens, I guess. I have to walk over, like I've done, and ask you to take a step back. Could you,
20 please? / Step back?

Evelyn: And if someone doesn't? / What then?

Adam: ... You're not gonna step back?

Evelyn: No ... I mean, yes, I probably will, but just for interest's sake, what would you do if?

---

1 miss [mɪs]: used to refer to a woman who is not married   **2** ms [mɪz]: used to refer to a woman who does not want it known if she is married or not   **3** s'pose (infml): suppose

Adam: I'm ... Geez, I'm not sure. I've never had anyone not step back. I've only said it, like, four times, and every time they've done it. Stepped back.

Evelyn: What if I'm your first? Non-stepper, I mean. Then what?

Adam: Hell, I dunno[1] ... I'm off in, like, ten minutes, I'd probably just   5
stand here, make sure you didn't touch anything.

Evelyn: Really?

Adam: Pretty much, yeah. I'd let next shift[2] talk to you, kick you out or whatever.

Evelyn: You wouldn't grab me or anything?   10

Adam: Nah. That's too ... you know. That's a total hassle[3], you end up rolling around on the ground, you'd probably sue[4] the place, or me, and then ... I'd get fired for doing my job. Screw that ... *(Beat[5].)* Could you do that for me, though?

Evelyn: Which, roll around on the ground or sue you?   15

Adam: No, step back behind the line there ... I'd appreciate it.

Evelyn: Not really.

Adam: No, seriously, I would. I'd definitely appreciate[6] it ...

Evelyn: I mean, 'not really' I'm not going to ...

Adam: I thought you just said you probably will ...   20

Evelyn: Yeah, 'probably'. I decided not to.

Adam: Hey, you're not gonna mess up my weekend with this, are you?

Evelyn: I wasn't planning on it, but ... I'm not completely against it, either.   25

Adam: See, if you get all crazy, then I gotta write up a report and stuff, I'm here till six, six-thirty easy, and I have a second job to get to.

Evelyn: Tonight? *Friday* night?

Adam: Yep. Right after this, at the video store ...   30

Evelyn: Why would anyone work two jobs on Friday night?

---

1 dunno (sl): I don't know   **2** shift: *Schicht*   **3** hassle: a situation that is annoying because it involves doing sth. difficult or complicated   **4** sue sb.: *jdn. verklagen*
5 beat (n): short pause   **6** appreciate sth.: be happy if sb. does sth. for you

Adam: ... For money.

Evelyn: Of course ... Sorry. *(Looks at him again.)* Oh ...Oh, right! That's where I ... I've seen you in there. You helped me once, I think.

5 **Adam:** Yeah? / With what?

Evelyn: Uh-huh. / *The Picture of Dorian Gray*[1]... You found it in classics, not drama. / Somebody'd misplaced it ...

Adam: Right, I remember that. / Yes ... Behind *Cabaret*[2]. The 'Joel Grey' fiasco ...

10 **Evelyn:** Yeah, you said you found it with *Dirty Dancing*[3] once, too, or something ...

Adam: I did, you're right ... That's funny.

Evelyn: Anyway, you helped me, that was nice ...

Adam: Thanks. But, you're not gonna return the favor, right?

15 **Evelyn:** You mean the ...?

She points back toward the velvet rope.

Adam: Yeah.

Evelyn: No, sorry, I can't.

Adam: Why is that? *(Pointing)* It's a pretty good-sized sculpture. You
20 can see it just fine from there ...

Evelyn: Truthfully? I'm building up my nerve, and if I go back over, I'll probably be a big wuss about it and take off ...

Adam: About what? The 'wuss[4]' part, I mean ...

Evelyn: I was going to deface[5] the statue.

25 **Adam:** Oh. Oh ... *(Pointing)* Is that paint?

Evelyn: Yes.

---

1 The Picture of Dorian Gray: movie adaption of the novel of the same name by Irish novelist and playwright Oscar Wilde (1854–1900)   **2** Cabaret: a musical (1972) starring Liza Minelli and Joel Grey about Berlin in the 1930s   **3** Dirty Dancing: American movie (1987) starring Patrick Swayze   **4** wuss (sl): a person who is not strong or brave   **5** deface sth.: damage the appearance of sth., esp. by drawing or writing on it

Adam: Great ... From across the room, I thought you were maybe one of the cleaning people, I was hoping that was lemon pledge[1] or something ...

They share a smile.

Paint's not really a great thing to have in a museum. People'll definitely take that the wrong way ...   5

Evelyn: How do they know which way to take it?

Adam: I'm thinking outside would be the general direction they'd steer[2] you with spray paint ... Why do you have that?

Evelyn: I was going to do something to the nude. Mess it up or ...   10

Adam: What, you mean, like, color it or something?

Evelyn: I was thinking more of painting a big dick on it, but whatever ...

Adam: Well, you could still color it in ... The dick[3].

Evelyn smiles at this.   15

Evelyn: True. It might look kinda weird ...

Adam: Oh, I think a graffiti penis is gonna be plenty odd already ... *(Beat.)* So, right over the leaves there, or just a free-floating[4] number?

Evelyn: Probably anatomically correct. I mean, if you're gonna do it,   20 why not –

Adam: – do it right? Absolutely. And, would 'why' be completely out of the question here?

Evelyn: Why the 'dick'?

Adam: Uh-huh. I mean, since I basically have to jump you now if   25 you lift that can up, it'd help with my report ...

Evelyn: Because I don't like art that isn't true.

Adam: 'True'. What do you mean?

Evelyn: False art. I hate it ...

---

1 lemon pledge: a cleaning product   **2** steer sb.: move sb. in a particular direction   **3** dick (sl): penis   **4** free-floating: not attached to anything

Other patrons[1] drift past. They watch them go.

Adam: No, I understand the words you've used there, although they're both pretty subjective. 'Art'. 'Truth'.

Evelyn: Exactly! That's the beauty of art ... It's subjective.

5 **Adam:** Right, but see, I don't know what you're referring to then. I mean, specifically ... *(Beat.)* Didn't Oscar Wilde say something like, 'In art there is no such thing as a universal truth ... ' or whatever?

Evelyn: Yes ... Very good. 'A truth in art is that whose contradictory

10 is also true'. Right, but that's an aesthetic[2]. I'm talking about practicalities. Censorship[3]. *(She points.)* This sculpture. It's fake, it's not real. Therefore, false art ...

Adam: No, it's a Fornecelli[4], it definitely is. I read the little thingie[5] there one time ...

15 **Evelyn:** Yes, but the leaf cluster isn't.

Adam: It's not? / What is it, a pastie[6] or something, like strippers have?

Evelyn: No. / It's plaster[7] ... It was added by a committee who had complaints from local townspeople. / Uh-huh. / They made a

20 petition and got that put on, thereby removing its subjectivity as art.

Adam: Really? / I didn't know that ... / When did they do this?

Evelyn: Seven or eight years ago now, I think. Before I got here, anyway. / See, they objected to his 'thing', the shape of it. Said

25 it was too life-like. *(Beat.)* It's supposed to be 'God', you know ... That's what pisses 'em off.

Adam: Huh. / Yeah ... He's not really supposed to have one of those, is he?

1 patron ['peɪtrən] (fml): (here) visitor   **2** aesthetic [es'θetɪk]: a point relating to the beauty of the item or issue in question   **3** censorship: the act of removing parts of a book, movie, etc. that are considered to be offensive, immoral or a political threat   **4** Fornecelli: fictional artist   **5** thingie (infml): thing; (here) label next to an artwork giving information about it   **6** pastie: (here) small round covering for a woman's nipples often worn a striptease performer **7** plaster: Gips

Evelyn: No, and I don't know why ... We're always calling him 'The Creator'. *(Beat.)* Look at it, you can see the ... See right behind the grapes there, you can just see his ...

Adam: ... Grapes. Yes. You're absolutely, huh. Didn't even cover him properly. Shoddy[1] craftsmanship! 5

Evelyn: I mean, if you're gonna do it, at least ...

Adam: ... Exactly. Do it right. *(Beat.)* But why deface the thing? I mean, just out of curiosity. Why not, say, knock the plaster off and expose his ... you know ... cluster ... if you're trying to ...

Evelyn: Because. That's so ... Expected. 10

Adam: Ahh ... So, you're a student, then, or is this just basic anarchy?

Evelyn: Yep. Student.

Adam: Me too.

Evelyn: Yeah? What's your emphasis?

Adam: Umm ... Taking out school loans[2], primarily, but I do sit in on 15
a few English classes. You're in art?

Evelyn: Mmm-hmm. M.F.A.[3] / Applied Theory and Crit[4].

Adam: Oh. / So, is this, like, a project?

Evelyn: No, I'm just getting started on my thesis[5] project now. A big sorta installation ... 'thingie'. 20

Adam: That's a good word, huh? 'Thingie'.

Evelyn: It is ... *(Points.)* Anyway, this is only a pet peeve[6]...

Adam: Thesis? You're graduating ...

Evelyn: In May.

Adam: 'Kay. I'm only a junior ... 25

Evelyn: Huh. You seem older.

Adam: Well, I am. I mean, older than twenty, anyhow ... I worked for a couple years. Made money.

Evelyn: Not enough, though. Still got two jobs ...

Adam: Don't forget the school loans ... 30

---

1 shoddy: made or done badly **2** school loan: money lent to a student to pay college fees **3** M.F.A.: Master of Fine Arts (college degree) **4** applied theory and crit(icism): *anwendungsorientierte Theorie und Kritik* **5** thesis ['θiːsɪs]: *Diplomarbeit* **6** pet peeve: sth. that annoys or bothers sb. a lot

Evelyn: Right. So, basically, you're … fucked.

Adam: Yep. But at least I'm educated, so I *comprehend* that I'm fucked …

They stand there for a moment. Adam checks his watch. Evelyn shakes her spray can.

Evelyn: You're cute. I don't like the way you wear your hair …

Adam: Thank you. I think …

Evelyn: No, you're definitely cute, but you shouldn't style it so much. Your hair. Just let it go …

Adam: 'Kay. I'll try that …

Evelyn: Your relief's[1] late …

Adam: Yeah. Typical …

Evelyn: So, do you have to stay at your station until they spell you, or …?

Adam: No, at punch-out time, I'm supposed to get down there and do it. They can really be pricks about that …

Evelyn: You should go then …

Adam: Right. Yeah, I … Can I call you?

Evelyn: What do you wanna call me?

Adam: Up. Just up, right now. Talk, maybe get crazy, take you to dinner …

Evelyn: Okay. Ahh … Sure. *(Beat.)* Do they allow you to do that here?

Adam: What, eat dinner?

Evelyn: I meant hit on[2] the patrons …

Adam: … Umm, no, they've got a pretty strict policy about that, too, actually. But …

Evelyn: … Ahh, the great equaliser. 'But.'

Adam: Exactly. I'll take the risk …

Evelyn: … Good answer, grasshopper[3].

Adam: Huh?

---

1 relief: person that takes the place of another on duty   **2** hit on sb.: start talking to sb. to show that you are sexually attracted   **3** grasshopper: *Heuschrecke*

Evelyn: *Kung Fu*[1] on TV. Remember when he was a kid? The old guy with the fakey contact lenses, and the …

Adam: Oh, right … Sure. 'Grasshopper.' I don't really watch much television …

Evelyn: My brothers loved that show. *(Beat.)* So, do you want a number?

Adam: Absolutely! *(Checks.)* Damn, I don't have a pen.

Evelyn: Me either. *(Thinks.)* Here …

Adam: What?

Evelyn: The jacket. Take it off for a second.

Adam: Oh, that's, umm …

Evelyn: What?

Adam: It's my own … 'S not part of the uniform. It's mine.

Evelyn: Good. Then you'll always have it on you … From the looks of it.

Adam follows her orders. Evelyn lays the coat open on the floor, looks around, then uncaps the paint and sprays a phone number inside.

… Don't worry, it dries quick.

Adam: Thanks. Okay, so, I'll … Yeah. *(He glances back.)* Good luck with the … Nice to meet you. Again.

Evelyn: You too.

Adam smiles at her, looks back again, walks off. Evelyn is left alone. She turns back to the statue and starts shaking her paint can. The little ball bearings[2] inside rattle loudly.

1 Kung Fu: popular TV series from the early 70s   **2** ball bearing: *Kugellager*

A RESTAURANT LOBBY

Adam standing with Evelyn. He looks a bit different, not as bulky, and he's letting his hair go. Same jacket under his arm.

Evelyn: ... No, seriously. You have.
Adam: Yeah?
5   **Evelyn:** No question.
Adam: I dunno. I think I still look ...
Evelyn: You can definitely tell. You can.
Adam: Really?
Evelyn: Definitely. Plus, the hair ... / I bet you your friends say
10   something. Twenty bucks[1] ...
Adam: Well, I'm glad ... / I mean, I can't tell and so I figured[2] ...
Twenty bucks?
Evelyn: Yes. That's because you see 'you' every day. Shower, getting
dressed, that kind of thing. But ...
15 **Adam:** So do you.
Evelyn: I don't see you shower. Or getting dressed ...
Adam: No, I meant every day. So far, anyway, since we first went
to ...
Evelyn: I know, I'm kidding.
20 **Adam:** Oh. Okay ... *(Beat.)* I'd like that, though. If you would ...
Evelyn: Which?
Adam: Both if you want. Either. Anything, any moment I can get
with you ... That's what I'd like.
Evelyn: Ask and you shall receive ...
25 **Adam:** So, I'm asking, then.
Evelyn: So you shall be receiving then ...

They share a brief kiss; he looks around self-consciously[3].

Adam: P.D.A. Public display of affection. I'm not used to that ...
Evelyn: No? I don't mind ...

1 buck (infml): US dollar   **2** figure: think   **3** self-conscious: *verunsichert*

Adam: Really?

Evelyn: Nah, whose business is it? Ours, right? Kiss if we want to, make love in the bathroom stall[1]... Who cares?

Adam: I'd start with the management ...

Evelyn: Yeah, but why should they? I mean ... We're two adults, we ...   5

Adam: I think this is a bigger discussion than before Jenny and Phillip get here ... / I mean, no, I'd love to have it with you, the discussion, and I agree, somewhat, but ...

Evelyn: Whatever. / I understand ...

Adam: Another time, we'll definitely discuss it.   10

Evelyn: Another time ... I'd rather do it.

Adam: Lemme go check the men's room ... *(He laughs.)* ... You amaze me.

Evelyn: I'm glad. *(Beat.)* And you amaze me, you do. Look at you!

Adam: ... It's just a little jogging.   15

Evelyn: No, it's not. It's not just that ... You're running, you're eating better, are you still lifting[2]?

Adam: Yeah ... I mean, I didn't today, but ...

Evelyn: That's okay.

Adam: No, I'm gonna ... So, yeah, alright, it's a whole routine thing.   20 You're right ...

Evelyn: Do you like doing it?

Adam: Honestly ... No. I totally hate it!

They laugh.

Evelyn: So why would you ...?   25

Adam: Because you suggested it. Which is kinda pathetic[3], but true ...

Evelyn: You shouldn't do something you don't wanna do.

Adam: Yeah, you should, why not? If it's for someone ... I mean, I'm doing it for you.   30

---

1 bathroom stall (AE): a small area in a public toilet surrounded by walls that contains a toilet   **2** lift: lift weights in a fitness studio or gym   **3** pathetic [pəˈθetɪk]: making you feel pity or sadness

Evelyn: It's a life change. Really …

Adam: Right.

Evelyn: I gave you a couple ideas and you're changing your entire life. I'm very proud of you.

5 **Adam:** Thank you … *(Cockney[1].)* 'Enry 'Iggins[2].

Evelyn: What's that? Who's …

Adam: Nothing. From a book. Play, actually.

Evelyn: Oh. *(Beat.)* Are you keeping your journal? It really does help …

10 **Adam:** Yes.

Evelyn: Will you let me read it?

Adam: … Some time.

Evelyn: Good.

They stand for a moment. Evelyn checks her watch.

15 **Adam:** And what about you?

Evelyn: What about me?

Adam: That's what I mean … I don't know.

Evelyn: What?

Adam: Nothing. I don't really know anything about you …

20 **Evelyn:** Yes, you do!

Adam: I don't. Not really …

Evelyn: What's my name?

Adam: Evelyn:.

Evelyn: Where am I from?

25 **Adam:** Illinois. Near Chicago?

Evelyn: Yes. How old am I?

Adam: Ummm … Twenty-five, maybe.

Evelyn: That's exactly right. Almost twenty-six. Sign?

Adam: Gemini[3], I think …

30 **Evelyn:** The twins, yes.

---

1 cockney: the dialect spoken by people from east London   **2** 'Enry 'Iggins: Henry Higgins, a character from G. B. Shaw's drama *Pygmalion* (1913)   **3** Gemini ['dʒemɪnaɪ]: *(Sternzeichen) Zwillinge*

Adam: Does that mean you have a split personality?

Evelyn: No, it means I was born in June.

Adam: Oh. *(Beat.)* And you're, what, a sculptress[1], right? An artist ...

Evelyn: Yep. Anything else you wanna know?

Adam: Yes ... Everything! 5

Evelyn: So ask then ...

Adam: Well ... Why are you always asking me questions if it's no big deal.

Evelyn: Because you make me curious ... I'm a curious person.

Adam: I'm curious, too, though! 10

Evelyn: Like I said ... So ask then.

Adam: ... Why do you like me?

Evelyn: What?

Adam: Me ... Why would you like me? I'm not anything, I mean ... And you're so ... 15

Evelyn: Don't do that, okay? That's the only thing about you I don't like ... What you see in yourself. Or don't see. Your insecurities. *(Beat.)* Do you like me?

Adam: Of course, you know I do ...

Evelyn: Do I appear to like you? Hmm? 20

Adam: Yes ... It seems like it, yeah.

Evelyn: I *do* like you. Do you think I'm smart?

Adam: I think you're amazing ... And you have a great ass. Just thought you should know ...

Evelyn: Not part of my query, but thank you. 25

Adam: Welcome ...

Evelyn: And do I seem to know my own mind? I mean, generally ...

Adam: No question.

Evelyn: So, don't you trust me, then, to know how I feel?

Adam: Yeah. No, you're right ... 30

Evelyn: Don't worry about *why* when *what* is right in front of you.

Adam: Those're very wise words from someone with such a great ass ...

1 sculptress: a woman that makes sculptures

Evelyn: *(Playfully)* Kiss me, grasshopper …

They start to kiss again as a young couple approaches.

Jenny: Ah, ah, ah … P.D.A.
Phillip: I don't think anybody wants to watch you kiss, Adam …
5   We'll be eating soon.
   Adam: Hey, Phillip, hello! Evelyn, this is Phillip, and his fiancée[1],
      Jenny …

'Hellos' all round.

Phillip: So, we should grab a table, and … *(Stopping to look)* Adam,
10   what's up with you? D'you lost weight?
   Adam: … A little, maybe.
   Jenny: No, he cut his hair … Or something. That's it, right?
   Adam: Umm, yeah. I mean, both, sort of.
   Phillip: Huh. Okay, so, let's … Come on.

15 *Jenny and Phillip lead the way. Evelyn stares at Adam as they follow;*
   he pulls a twenty out of his pocket and places it in her hand.

---

1 fiancée [ˌfiːɑːnˈseɪ]: a woman who is engaged to be married to a man

A LIVING ROOM

Adam and Evelyn sitting on a couch. Jenny and Phillip in opposing chairs. Everyone holds a drink.

Adam: ... So, tell me this again, you're going to what?

Phillip: Underwater. We're going to get married underwater ...

Adam: You've gotta be kidding me!   5

Phillip: ... Like those *Life*[1] magazine photos you see or whatever. Seriously.

Jenny: We wanted to try something bold ...

Evelyn: That oughta[2] do it.

Adam: This is crazy, really. And, so, if we want to attend we have   10
to ...

Phillip: ... Get in the tank with us. You bet.

Jenny: No, honey, I thought we said ...

Phillip: ... We haven't, okay, no, we haven't settled[3] that part
completely, but ...   15

Jenny: My dad could never do that. I mean, my mom would try, she
would, but Dad ...

Phillip: Maybe people can watch from the glass window things or
whatever, but I'd prefer if they came in with us ...

He drains his glass, looking at Adam.   20

Adam: That is nuts ...

Evelyn: I applaud you. I think it's very ...

Phillip: *(To Evelyn)* Yeah, well, don't expect my buddy here to follow
in our footsteps. He's the least adventurous person I know ...

Evelyn: Really?   25

Phillip: Absolutely! And the marriage thing? Uh-uh, not gonna
happen, sorry. I don't know how many nights I listened to this
guy say, 'Not me, man, I'm never getting hooked[4], no way, man ...'

---

1 Life: popular magazine (1936–2007)   **2** oughta (infml): ought to   **3** settle sth.:
agree on sth.   **4** get hooked (infml): get married

Evelyn: Is that right? Well, well …
Adam: Listen, don't encourage him. My room-mate doesn't need any –
Phillip: Former room-mate …
5 **Adam:** – more encouragement. *(Beat.)* I'm gonna look stupid in one of those wet suits.
Phillip: Hey, let's not be a party pooper[1] here, my friend … This could've been you.

Adam laughs thinly; Evelyn doesn't understand.

10 **Adam:** I know, I know …
Phillip: Right?
Evelyn: I'm lost. What's …?
Phillip: I stole Jenny away from Adam …
Adam: Come on …
15 **Phillip:** I did! *(To Jenny)* Didn't I?
Jenny: No, you didn't, stop being … *(To Evelyn)* Adam and I had a class together, but he never got up the nerve to ask me out.
Evelyn: Is that true?
Adam: Something like that …
20 **Jenny:** Four months we sat next to each other – I'm borrowing his pen, like, all the time, hint-hint – and he's this total monk the whole semester … Anyway, Phil picks him up from class one day, sees me, and we went to the movies that same night.
Phillip: I cannot tell a lie … I've got the moves[2], God help me.
25 **Adam:** God help all of us …

A collective laugh.

Evelyn: Well, like I said, I think it's great. It's really amazing, it is, to find anybody willing to take a risk today. To look a little silly or different or anything. Bravo! *(Toasts[3].)* To people with balls …

---

1 party pooper: a person who spoils the fun for other people   **2** have the moves (infml): know how to chat up a girl   **3** toast sb./sth.: *jdn./etwas anstoßen*

They all toast, even Phillip with his empty glass, but he looks over at Adam. Adam blushes.

Phillip: 'Balls', huh? Yep, that's my Jenny …

Jenny slaps him on the shoulder and blushes again.

Evelyn: You know what I mean. Guts. That kinda thing …   5
Jenny: Right. I got it.
Phillip: *(Toasting)* 'To balls, long may they wave …'

They all smile and mock-drink again.

I'll tell you what took some balls, the museum thing, a few weeks
back, with the … balls. You guys read about that?! I mean, Adam,   10
of course you did, you work there, but – Evelyn, you hear about
it?
Jenny: *(Whispering)* The penis …
Evelyn: *(Whispering)* Yes, I did. Why are we whispering?
Phillip: Because you don't say 'penis' in Jenny's house. But we're at   15
my place now, and so we sing it from the eaves[1]! 'Penis!! Penis!!!'
Adam: Okay, bar's closing, last call …
Evelyn: I'm an artist, so I didn't …
Phillip: No, seriously, do you believe that shit? Somebody with the
gall[2] to do that kinda bullshit on our campus?! That fucking   20
burns me up[3] …
Adam: We should probably get, umm …
Phillip: … What does that mean, anyway? 'I'm an artist'?
Evelyn: It means nothing, really, just that I understand the impulse …
Phillip: You what?!   25
Adam: Evelyn, maybe we should …
Phillip: No, wait Adam, I wanna hear … What 'impulse?' it's called
'vandalism'.
Jenny: Does anyone want dessert?

---

1 eaves (pl): the lower edges of a roof that stick out over the walls   **2** gall: rude
behavior showing a lack of respect that is surprising because the person
behaving badly is not embarrassed   **3** burn sb. up (infml): make sb. angry

Phillip holds up a hand to hush the group. He turns back to Evelyn.

Phillip: No, hold on, this is rich[1]. Go ahead …

Evelyn: Just that … I don't think it was just kids playing. I think it was a sort of statement, a kind of …

5 **Phillip:** … A statement?

Evelyn: Yeah, I do …

Jenny: What kind of statement would that be? It was pornography …

Evelyn: No, it wasn't.

Jenny: Yes, it was …

10 **Evelyn:** Pornography is meant to titillate[2], to excite you. Did you see a picture of what happened?

Phillip: We did, yeah …

Evelyn: Does a penis excite you? I mean, just any ol' penis?

Phillip: You're funny. And that's not the point.

15 **Evelyn:** It's totally the point … How about you, Jenny, did you like what you saw? Did it get you hot?

Phillip: This is, like, uncalled for, okay? All she said was …

Evelyn: I know what she said, why don't you let her speak? *(To Jenny)* Did you wanna say anything else? Huh? Okay, then … All

20 I'm saying is that, in my *opinion,* it wasn't pornography, it was a statement. Of course, that's the beauty of statements, like art, they're subjective. You and I can think completely different things and we can both be right … Unless, and this seems quite probable, you just can't stand to lose an argument.

25 *Quiet for a moment from the group.*

Phillip: Wow. The postgraduate[3] mind at work …

Adam: I'll help you get dessert, Jenny, if you want to …

Jenny: … I still don't think that makes it a statement. It's graffiti …

Evelyn: What do you mean, it would be a huge statement …

30 Especially for a town like this.

---

1 rich (infml): very interesting   **2** titillate sb.: interest or excite sb., esp. in a sexual way   **3** postgraduate: a person who already holds a first degree and who is doing advanced study or research

Phillip: Hey, some of us are from 'a town like this', so maybe you should watch it.

Evelyn: Well, we've all gotta be from somewhere ...

Phillip: What do you mean by that?

Evelyn: I mean, it's a little college town in the middle of nowhere and ...   5

Phillip: One you chose, presumably ...

Evelyn: No, it chose me, actually. *Full* scholarship[1]. So, as I was saying ...

Phillip: You've got a real winning[2] way, you know that?   10

Adam: Look, Phil, it's no big deal, let's just ...

Phillip: Which 'Take Back the Night' rally[3] did you find her at, Adam?

Evelyn: ... Can I finish, please?! Jesus, you're really the obnoxious[4] type, you know that? *(To Adam)* How long did you have to   15 stomach[5] this guy?

Everyone except Evelyn sort of freezes on that one.

Adam: Evelyn.

Evelyn: Anyhow, who knows what the person was saying by it, we don't, but I think it was a gesture. A kind of manifesto[6], if you   20 will ...

Phillip: *(Drily)* I don't think a person's dick can be a manifesto. Uh-uh. You can write a manifesto on your thing, but your thing can't be one ... I'm sure I read that somewhere.

Evelyn: See? You're just trying to be ...   25

---

1 scholarship: an amount of money given to sb. by an organization to help pay for their education   2 winning (adj): attractive in a way that makes other people like you   3 take the night back rally: an event held to stop sexual and domestic violence   4 obnoxious [əbˈnɑkʃəs]: extremely unpleasant, esp. in a way that offends people   5 stomach sb./sth.: like sb./sth.   6 manifesto: written statement in which a group of people, esp. a political party, explain their beliefs and future action

Phillip: I'm not trying to be anything! Who the hell do you think you are, a few double dates and telling me anything about who I am? Un-fucking-believable!

Jenny: This is getting a little, ahh …

5 **Phillip:** … Adam, you can really pick 'em. Wow, man!

Adam: Look, it's not, let's just forget the …

Evelyn: You're not gonna take his side in this, are you?

Adam: I'm not taking sides, I'm trying to get outta here with just a touch[1] of dignity, okay? Jesus …

10 **Jenny:** I've got a test tomorrow, anyway …

Phillip: 'Statement', she says!

Evelyn: Shut the fuck up, alright? Just fuck right off … How would you know? I think she was making one, so that's my opinion …

Adam: Jenny, thanks for everything. Phillip, I'll call ya, or whatever,
15 but we're gonna …

Phillip: Yeah? How do you know it was a girl?

Evelyn: … I don't. I didn't say it was a woman.

Phillip: Girl, woman, whatever. You said 'she', how do you know that?

20 **Evelyn:** I don't, I just said. It's a guess. What it was, where it was placed. An *educated* guess …

Phillip: You are not … She's not trying to take a poke[2] at my being an undergrad[3], is she? Adam, tell me she didn't just …

Jenny: Can we stop, now, please?! You guys …

25 **Adam:** Evelyn, let's go …

Phillip: Hey, artiste … How'd you know it was a woman who painted the cock, huh? Very, very suspicious there …

Evelyn: You are such a prick, man, how do you go on, day after day? *(To Adam)* Let's go …

30 *She rises, snatches up her things and moves toward the door.*

---

1 a touch: a small amount   **2** take a poke at sb./sth.: make an unkind remark about sb./sth.   **3** undergrad (infml): undergraduate; student who is studying for their first degree at university

Adam? Are you coming?

Adam: I'm ... Yeah, but, just go. I'll meet you downstairs, I just wanna ... Go ahead.

Evelyn: 'Kay. *(To Jenny)* You're very sweet. Good luck ... I don't think that's gonna be enough, but I still wish it on you.   5

She heads for the door and exits.

Phillip: 'Good luck.' Hey, fuck you! *(To Adam)* Where in hell did you meet that bitch?! / What'd she do, give you a haircut and a blow job and now you're her puppy?!! / You don't have to go ...

Adam: ... At the museum. / No, I'm not her ... / *(To Jenny)* The 10 wedding sounds great. Really ... It sounds ... Yeah.

He wanders off. Phillip and Jenny sit in silence.

Phillip: ... What?

A BEDROOM

Adam and Evelyn in bed. Holding each other, staring off. A video camera on a tripod[1] nearby.

Evelyn: ... Umm, nice.

5 **Adam:** Very. Yes.

Evelyn: Our bodies are beginning to understand one another ...

Adam: You're right, I mean ...

Evelyn: Getting a rhythm. And less inhibited[2].

Adam: Yep.

10 *He leans over and whispers something in her ear. A huge smile across her face. She turns and whispers back to him. They laugh and kiss for a moment. They hold one another.*

Evelyn: *(Quietly)* Were you always like this before? So ... You know ...

Adam: ... Shy? Just about the fact that no one would sleep with me.

15 That's all.

Evelyn: Come on ...

Adam: Seriously. You're only, like, I dunno, the third person I've ever ...

Evelyn: ... No ...

20 **Adam:** Yes, I mean it. And they were both young. I mean, I was too, I wasn't, like, hanging out at a *daycare* or anything, but ... It was during high school mostly. So ... You're sort of in uncharted[3] waters here.

Evelyn: I don't wanna blow[4] your cover but ... I could kinda tell.

25 **Adam:** *(Smiling)* Yeah? Well, that's okay ...

Evelyn: And nobody here at school?

Adam: Nothing serious. Dates. Some close calls. But not anyone ... You know.

Evelyn: ... Like Jenny.

---

1 tripod ['traɪpɒd]: a support with three legs for a camera   **2** inhibited: unable to relax or express your feelings in a natural way   **3** uncharted: not familiar
4 blow your cover: (here) show that you know the real story

Adam: No.

Evelyn: You sorry you didn't ask her out? I mean, if I wasn't in the
equation[1] ...

Adam: Not really. We just never got the right ... Whatever. I sorta
blew that one. Anyway, it's kind of weird talking about ...   5

Evelyn: It's okay. That's nice to see, every so often. Someone
gallant[2] ...

Adam: Which is medieval for 'loser' ... *(Beat.)* I wanna tell you
something – and this is not because we've been sleeping
together or because you mentioned another girl, it's not – I can't   10
stop thinking about you. I can't. I mean, it's not like a stalker[3]
situation ... Yet ... But I'm finding myself hanging out by your
classes. Following you ...

Evelyn: I've noticed ...

Adam: I figured, yeah. And taking my jacket off, like, thirty times a   15
day and looking at your number. Staring at it. Wondering if you're
looking at my number. And writing your name on anything!
All over my books. In my *food*. Seriously, tracing your name in
whatever I'm eating. I'm so whipped[4] ... You are dangerously
close to owning me.   20

Evelyn: Wow ...

Adam: I just signed my relationship death warrant[5] didn't I? What
a dork[6] ...

Evelyn: ... No, it's sweet. *(Beat.)* Were you nervous tonight? I mean,
about us with the ...   25

Adam: Nah. Not really. A bit.

Evelyn: Sure?

Adam: Yeah. It's just ... Let's not watch it, okay? Do we have to do
that?

---

1 equation: *Gleichung*   **2** gallant: giving polite attention to women   **3** stalker: a
person who follows and watches another person over a long period of time in a
way that is annoying or frightening   **4** be whipped (infml): be completely
controlled by your lover   **5** death warrant: official document stating that sb.
should receive the punishment of being killed for a crime   **6** dork (AE infml): a
stupid or boring person that other people laugh at

Evelyn: Not if you don't want to …

Adam: Good. I don't think I could get into that, actually.

Evelyn: Why not? It'd be fun …

Adam: I don't really need to see myself doing that. Doing … stuff.

5 **Evelyn:** See, I'm totally different. I think everyone should see themselves doing it, and their friends should see it, too.

Adam: And that's why the tape's gonna stay at my place …

She smiles at this, kissing him.

Evelyn: Don't be so frightened of everything.

10 **Adam:** I'm not. Not frightened, anyway. I just don't think that's a thing other people need to see. Ever. My ass …

Evelyn: People like who … Phillip?

Adam: No, that's fine, you can show it to him … *(Beat.)* Are you nuts?!

Evelyn: Why is he your friend?

15 **Adam:** Do you really wanna go over that …?

Evelyn: I just don't get it.

Adam: What's to get? We were room-mates, we occasionally see each other, have a drink …

Evelyn: I just don't think you need that kind of person in your life.
20 No one does.

Adam: *(Mock-serious)* … It may be a touch early to start dictating who my friends are.

Evelyn: *(With charm)* Yeah … I s'pose.

Adam: Geez, he really got under your skin, didn't he?

25 **Evelyn:** Under. Over. Around. I hate that kind of guy …

Adam: What kind?

Evelyn: That kind. Whatever he is, that's what I hate …

Adam: I'll let him know.

Evelyn: No, God, no, don't give him the satisfaction. And he'd take it,
30 too, believe me …

Adam: Nah, maybe it'd help him, you know, be better … Or something.

Evelyn: The only thing that would help him is a fucking knife through his throat …

They grow quiet for a moment. Adam studies Evelyn.

Adam: Okay, I'm glad I don't have a pet rabbit[1] or anything right now ...

Evelyn: *(Laughing)* You know what I mean.

Adam: Umm, no, not really.   5

Evelyn: I've just been around his type, that's all. And I don't like 'em.

Adam: Yeah, I got that part[2] ...

Evelyn: No big deal.

Adam: Right, no, it was the 'knife through the throat' part that was the big deal, I thought ...   10

Evelyn: Oh, that's just an expression.

Adam: ... From where, Transylvania[3]?

She kisses him.

Evelyn: No ... From the 'Scorned[4] Girl's Handbook'.

Adam: Ahhh. Right ... Page 666.   15

Evelyn: *(Smiling)* You've been peeking[5]. You know what happens to peekers, don't you?

Adam: Well, if they're DJs, they usually get asked to play 'Misty'[6] on the radio all the time ...

Evelyn: Close. No, I'll show you ... But you have to do me a favor.   20

Adam: What's that?

She starts to slip under the covers.

Evelyn: ... Just smile. Smile into the camera. For as long as you can ...

---

1 pet rabbit: reference to the film *Fatal Attraction* (1987) in which a jealous woman boils the pet rabbit of her lover   **2** get that part (infml): understand sth.
3 Transylvania: region in Romania, known as the home of Dracula   **4** scorned: when your partner has betrayed you   **5** peek: look at sth. quickly and secretly
6 play 'misty': reference to the thriller *Play Misty for Me* (1971), in which a radio DJ (played by Clint Eastwood) is stalked by a female fan, who always asks him to play the song Misty

A PARK

Jenny waiting on a bench. Sitting by herself. After a moment, Adam appears.

Adam: ... Hey.

5 **Jenny:** Adam, hi, hello.

Adam: Hi.

Jenny: Thanks for coming, I appreciate it.

Adam: Of course. How's it going?

Jenny: You know ... Okay.

10 **Adam:** Right.

Jenny: Lots to do for a wedding.

Adam: I'll bet ...

Jenny: Invitations to get out, arrangements to make ...

Adam: ... Air tanks to fill ...

15 *Jenny laughs lightly.*

Jenny: That too.

Adam: So, you guys're still going through with that?

Jenny: That's what we're saying ...

Adam: What do you mean, 'saying'?

20 **Jenny:** No, we are, it's what we're doing, I'm just ...

Adam: ... Jenny, what?

Jenny: I don't know. I'm, you know, worried.

Adam: Why? About what?

Jenny: What do you think? Phillip. He's just ... I dunno, being funny.

25 **Adam:** Funny, how? Like 'telling jokes' funny or 'making letter bombs' funny?

Jenny: No, no bombs yet, but kind of ... Just funny. Odd. *(Beat.)* Like, nice ...

Adam: 'Nice'?

30 **Jenny:** Yeah, you know ... Sweet. Now, I love him and all, I do, you know that, but that's not the way I'd describe him to people. 'Sweet.' Would you?

Adam thinks for a moment.

Adam: No, I wouldn't exactly use his name and 'sweet' in the same
short story ...

Jenny: And that's what's bugging[1] me.

Adam: Why, though? Maybe he's just ...   5

Jenny: I've only seen him like this once before, maybe twice.
Definitely once, when we were first going out and he was seeing
somebody else, too. It was over, mostly, but he was still seeing
her. Remember that?

Adam: ... Yeah. I do. The 'other' one.   10

Jenny: The other Jenny, exactly. I'd call and I could hear him freeze
up, stop for a moment if he answered and I said, 'Hey, it's Jenny.'
He didn't know what to do, so he'd get all sort of sweet and fish
around[2] slowly until he figured out if it was her or me ... God, I
used to hate that!   15

Adam: So, do you know anyone else named 'Jenny' right now?

Jenny: No, I don't mean that, not the name so much as the feeling ...
That sense that there's someone else.

Adam: Nah ...

Jenny: Maybe I'm making it up, you know, my own insecurities and   20
looking for a reason to not ...

Adam: *(Smiling)* ... Dive in? Take the plunge[3]? Jump off the deep
end[4]? Stop me before I ...

Jenny: Cute ... But yes. And that might be it, but I don't think so. I
want to get married, I do, and I love the guy, whether he's sweet   25
or not. It's just that I don't believe him now that he is ...

Adam: Well, you got[5] me ...

Jenny: Really? You don't know anything, haven't felt that or ...

---

1 bug sb. (infml): annoy or irritate sb.   **2** fish around: (here) try and find out
information   **3** take the plunge (infml): decide to do sth. important or difficult,
esp. after thinking about it for a long time   **4** jump off the deep end: start or be
made to start a new and difficult activity that you are not prepared for   **5** get sb.
(infml): make sb. confused because they do not know sth.

Adam: I only see him, like, once a week in our survey course[1], so it's not like I'm in the inner circle any more …

Jenny: I know, I just thought that …

Adam: … But I would tell you, Jenny, I would, seriously.

5 **Jenny:** Really?

Adam: I think so … I mean, that's a lousy thing to pass on to a person, and if I did, you know, know something and then told you, you'd more likely hate me forever than be grateful …

Jenny: Yeah, that's probably true …

10 **Adam:** Umm, you could lie, you know, feel free.

Jenny: No, you're probably right …

Adam: So, that doesn't exactly make me want to come clean[2] here – which I don't have anything to come clean about, okay, honestly, I just mean, whatever – But I feel I would. I do, because I think

15 you're pretty amazing, if the truth be known, and you're almost married so why shouldn't it be? The truth, I mean.

Jenny: … Thank you.

Adam: Not a problem. Anyway, that's all I know. Which is, nothing …

Jenny: 'Kay. I'm just being stupid.

20 **Adam:** Look, if you feel it, it's not stupid …

Jenny studies him hard.

Jenny: You're a lovely person, you know that?

Adam: 'Lovely'? Jesus, why don't you just call me 'gay' and get it over with?

25 **Jenny:** Hey, 'lovely' is nice … I wish there were a few more 'lovely' people in the world. I mean it, you are. *(Looks at him again.)* And getting cuter by the day. What is that girl doing to you?

Adam: Lots … She's amazing, really.

Jenny: What happened to your … Are you wearing … Adam, are

30 those contacts[3]?

---

1 survey course: an introductory course at a university   **2** come clean with sb. about sth.: admit and explain sth. that you have kept as a secret   **3** contacts: contact lenses

Adam: Yeah. Contacts.

Jenny: My God, this from the former 'tape around the nose thingie[1]'champion …

Adam: That was only for a week, that one time!

Jenny: Still, you've gotta admit … 5

Adam: I do, it's amazing. I feel better …

Jenny: Better? You're, like, this totally hot guy now … *(Beat.)* I always thought you were handsome, anyway, but I didn't think you'd go in for the makeover thing[2].

Adam: Me either. Who knew? 10

Jenny: Well, apparently she did … *(Beat.)* You are still seeing her, aren't you?

Adam: Oh yeah. She's … You don't hold a grudge[3], all she said that night at your … God, I couldn't believe that!

Jenny: It was great. No, truthfully, it was, Phil needed to hear every 15 word of that and he did, too. Hear it, I mean. Even said something after you guys left that night. Not an admittance of guilt, exactly, but as close to one as we're likely to hear from the guy …

Adam: Really, what'd he say? I'm amazed …

Jenny: As was I … He put on quite the show … 20

Adam: *(Sarcastically)* Yeah, I remember vaguely … They both did.

Jenny: Right, but later he said something like, 'He could do worse.'

Adam: Not exactly a seal of approval[4] …

Jenny: No, but a lot. For him. And after what she said …

Adam: You're right. Huh. 25

Jenny: Hey … Her middle name's not 'Jenny' or anything, is it?

Adam laughs at this.

---

1 tape around the nose thingie: reference to glasses that are broken and held together by tape   **2** makeover thing: reference to when people completely change their looks, style of clothing, etc. in order to look and feel better   **3** hold a grudge against sb.: feel anger or dislike towards sb. because that person has done sth. bad to you in the past   **4** seal of approval: action or statement that shows that sb. likes sth.

Adam: Nah, no such luck. It's 'Ann.' Evelyn Ann Thompson. Nice, right?

Jenny: Eat.

Adam: Huh?

5 **Jenny:** 'EAT'. Those're her initials, the acronym of her names. E-A-T.

Adam: Hey, that's cute ...

Jenny: Oh God, you're a goner[1].

Adam: I know, it's pathetic, isn't it?

Jenny: Yeah, somewhat ... But lovely.

10 **Adam:** Not that again ...

He puts a hand up to hide his face. Jenny grabs one of his hands, studying it.

Jenny: What the heck[2] is this? What is this?!

Adam: What ...?

15 **Jenny:** Did you stop biting your nails?

Adam: Yeah, for, like, a month now ...

Jenny: Don't tell me ...

Adam: It's true. She put some crap on them, slapped 'em out of my mouth a few times and that was it. I stopped ...

20 **Jenny:** You have nails! This is crazy ...

Adam: It's no big ...

Jenny: Ever since I've known you, three years now, your fingers've looked like raw meat ... Anyway, awful. And now you just quit?! This girl is the Messiah[3].

25 **Adam:** I've quit before ...

Jenny: For, like, an hour! *(Beat.)* I love this woman ...

Adam: Me too.

Jenny: Yeah, I see that. Wow ... *(She looks over at Adam again.)* And you'd really tell me if you knew something?

30 **Adam:** ... I would. Yes.

1 goner (infml): person who cannot be saved from a dangerous situation
2 what the heck? (infml): expression of surprise   **3** messiah [mə'saɪə]: person who saves your life or soul

Jenny: 'Kay. Damn, when did you get so cute?

She kisses him lightly on the cheek. They look at each other for a long moment. Suddenly, they kiss. A real kiss, not a 'Great to see you, aren't we the best of friends' kiss. After a moment, they shudder to a halt[1].

Adam: ... Shit.   5

Jenny: Yeah. Huh.

Adam: What was that all about?

Jenny: I dunno. I just ... I'm not sure.

Adam: Look, I'm sorry.

Jenny: No, don't be. I am. I'm the one with the ring on ...   10

Adam: Yeah, good point. My friend's ring. Thanks for reminding me ...

Jenny: Welcome.

Adam: Oh, God ... Damn it!

Jenny: ... No, listen. It wasn't because of, you know, my worries or   15
whatever. How I feel about Phillip right now. It wasn't ...

Adam: Okay.

Jenny: It just –

Adam: – happened.

Jenny: Right. I've wanted to do that for a long time ... Three years ...   20

Adam: ... Me too. *(Beat.)* And now we take it out in the woods and
bury it ... Don't we?

Jenny: Yeah. I mean, yes, definitely. I guess ...

Adam: Don't you think? We have to ... Jesus, what're we even talking
about?!   25

Jenny: No, we do. Course. Don't you want to?

Adam: Bury it?

Jenny: Yes ... Or ...

Adam: No, we can't talk about ... Don't even say the ... Do you have
a shovel[2] in your car?   30

Jenny: I don't, no ... But I have my car.

---

1 shudder to a halt: stop in a shaking movement   **2** shovel: tool needed to dig a hole

Adam: … My bike's right over there.

Jenny: Is it locked up?

Adam: Uh-huh.

Jenny: Then it should be fine …

5 **Adam:** I suppose so. It's a small town, after all.

Jenny: That's what people say …

Adam: Good people. People we know and care about …

Jenny: Right. *(Beat.)* Come on, we should go bury this. In the woods …

10 *They kiss again, then stand up slowly and walk off. She puts an arm through his.*

A DOCTOR'S LOUNGE

Adam and Evelyn sit on opposing couches, flipping through magazines. After a moment, he glances up and checks his watch.

Adam: What time did they say?

Evelyn: Like, ten-thirty …

Adam: And it's ten-fifty now …   5

Evelyn: No big deal, you always wait at the doctor's office.

Adam: I know, I just have to be at work by twelve.

Evelyn: Today?

Adam: Yeah, I told you that …

Evelyn: No, you didn't.   10

Adam: I did … I always work Wednesdays.

Evelyn: Really?

Adam: Yeah, every Wednesday.

Evelyn: Damn. I hope they …

Adam: It's okay. I guess I could be a little late if I have to …   15

Evelyn: Sure?

Adam: Uh-huh. It's alright … I mean, they hate it but I can make something up.

Evelyn: We can go.

Adam: No, I wanna do this. I do … *(Beat.)* Who wouldn't want to get   20
their nose chopped off[1]?

Evelyn: Come on! It's not …

Adam: I'm kidding. No, I think you're right about it …

Evelyn: It's just shaving it …

Adam: Yeah, that's much better. 'Shaving' your nose off … That   25
settles the nerves.

Evelyn: You're only talking to them, anyway, that's all.

Adam: I know, it's just weird to think …

Evelyn: People do it all the time.

---

1 chop sth. off: cut sth. off

Adam: Right, no, you're right, I just never imagined myself one of those people ...

Evelyn: I'm one of those people. Would you ever've guessed that?

Adam: What? You are not ...

5 **Evelyn:** Bullshit. Take a look ...

Adam: Where ...? *(He moves over to her, studies her nose.)* I don't see anything.

Evelyn: Exactly.

Adam: You had your nose done? Honestly?

10 **Evelyn:** At sixteen. My parents' birthday present ...

Adam: Thoughtful ...

Evelyn: No, I asked for it. I had this terrible hook[1]. 'The Jewish slope[2]' we called it in Lake Forest ... The only ski run for miles around!

Adam: *(Smiling)* I can't believe it ... I can't tell ...

15 **Evelyn:** That's the idea, isn't it?

Adam: Yeah, but ... You could be lying to me.

Evelyn: And what would be the point of that?

Adam: To get me in here. To watch chunks[3] of my flesh get torn away ... You could be a sadist[4], for all I know ...

20 **Evelyn:** Hey, quit sweet-talking[5] me ...

Adam: Well, they did an amazing job. *(Beat.)* Wait a minute, your name's 'Thompson', that's not Jewish ...

Evelyn: On my mother's side, you dope. That's what makes me Jewish ... Her maiden name is 'Tessman'.

25 **Adam:** Oh.

Evelyn: We don't have to stay here, Adam: ...

Adam: No, it's alright, it just makes me a little jumpy ...

Evelyn: It's cosmetic, not corrective ... It's no big deal. I promise ...

---

1 hook (n): a curved piece of metal, e.g. for hanging clothes or catching fish
2 Jewish slope: large curved nose (believed to be typically Jewish)   **3** chunk: piece   **4** sadist: person that enjoys seeing others suffer   **5** sweet-talk (v): say nice things to sb. in order to persuade that person to do sth.

Adam: If it's cosmetic, why can't I just put some powder on it or something, or shade it in on the side like they do for Richard Gere in photos ...

Evelyn: You mean, before?

Adam: ... He had it done?!   5

Evelyn: Take a look at *American Gigolo*[1] and then at any picture of him today. I'm serious. Lots of guys do it ... Joel Grey.

Adam: Okay, that's it, let's go ...

Evelyn: *(Laughing)* Kidding! What about Sting?

Adam: Yeah, I knew he did. Looked totally different in *Quadrophenia*[2].   10 I used to rent that video all the time, my 'mod'[3] phase ...

Evelyn: That must've been cute ... *(Beat.)* Does he look better now? Sting, I mean?

Adam: I suppose so ... Maybe it's just all that yoga, though.

Evelyn: I think you'll look great. You have a good face, a nice shape   15 to your nose, actually, but it's just got that bit of ...

Adam: What?

Evelyn: ... Bulb[4] ... At the end. Not a bulb, exactly, but ...

Adam: No, I got it, sort of the 'Rudolph' effect[5]. At least I can guide your sleigh[6] tonight ...   20

Evelyn: You can guide my sleigh any night.

They look at one another, kiss.

Adam: P.D.A.

Evelyn: Indeed ...

Adam: Shall I check the men's room?   25

Evelyn: I dare[7] you ...

Adam: Shut up!

---

1 American Gigolo: film (1980) starring Richard Gere as a male escort
2 Quadrophenia: film (1979) about mods and rockers starring Sting   **3** mod: member of a 1960s youth movement in Britain who wore neat, fashionable clothes and rode motor scooters   **4** bulb: *Glühbirne*   **5** 'Rudolph' effect: reference to Rudolph, the red-nosed Reindeer, who according to a song had a very shiny nose   **6** sleigh [sleɪ]: *Schlitten*   **7** dare sb.: persuade sb. to do sth. dangerous so that they can show that they are not afraid

Evelyn: I'm serious ...

Adam: You're crazy ...

Evelyn: Quite possibly. I still dare you ...

Adam: What if they call us?

5 **Evelyn:** Then they'll just have to wait, won't they?

Adam: I suppose they would ...

Evelyn: Can you afford to be late, that's the question. Will you take the risk ...?

Adam: Is this, like, my last meal or something? A conjugal[1] visit

10 before I'm drawn and quartered[2] ...

Evelyn: Stop being so morbid[3] ... It's just flesh.

Adam: Yeah, I see what you mean ... 'It's just flesh,' that's not morbid at all.

Evelyn: It isn't. It's one of the most perfect substances on earth.

15 Natural, beautiful. Think about it ...

Adam: I'd rather not.

Evelyn: Oh come on ... You've bitten more skin off from around your fingernails than a doctor would ever trim[4] off your nose. It's true ...

20 **Adam:** Yeah, but that's just ...

Evelyn: ... What? It's the same thing. Now, that grows back and this wouldn't, but that's about the only difference. *(Beat.)* How did you get that scar on your back?

Adam: Which, the ...?

25 **Evelyn:** Yes. The raised one ...

Adam: A kid, umm, threw a stick at me ... First grade.

Evelyn: Stitches?

Adam: Yeah. Thirty-three ...

Evelyn: And is that terrible? Are you disfigured[5] because of it ...?

30 **Adam:** Well, I don't like to wear tanktops ...

---

1 conjugal visit ['kɑndʒəgl]: visit of a married partner to his / her spouse in prison, during which sex is allowed   **2** draw and quarter sb.: *(Hinrichtungsmethode) jdn. ausweiden und vierteilen*   **3** morbid: thinking of death   **4** trim sth.: cut off little pieces of sth.   **5** disfigure sb.: spoil the appearance of sb.

Evelyn: ... And you should be respected for that.

Adam: *(Giggling)* I'm serious ... It bugs me ...

Evelyn: Okay, but why? Because it looks ugly or because you think other people will think it looks bad? Which?

Adam: I dunno ...

Evelyn: What's the matter with scars? Not a thing ... *(Pulls up sleeve.)* Look at these, see there?

Adam: What're those?

Evelyn: They're scars ... Lots of little scars. You didn't notice them before?

Adam: Yeah, I guess I did, but I didn't think anything ...

Evelyn: Sure, you did. Of course you would, they're on my wrist. You know what they are ...

Adam: ... Did you try to ...?

Evelyn: No, not really. I mean, I cut on myself a little, tried to get attention when I was a teenager, but I didn't want to slit my veins open. Or I would have ...

Adam: Oh.

Evelyn: I'm a very straightforward person.

Adam: Yeah, I'm getting that ...

Evelyn: It's the only way to be. Why lie?

Adam: You're right.

Evelyn: Exactly. *(Beat.)* So, is my arm unattractive to you, then, because of those, or not? Tell me ...

Adam: No ...

Evelyn: Are you lying?

Adam: No, not at all, I love your arm.

Evelyn: 'Love' is a big word ...

Adam: I know that. That's why I used it. I don't throw it around, believe me ...

Evelyn: Either do I.

Adam: I love your arm. It's beautiful ...

He takes hold of her wrist gently, kisses it.

Evelyn: They're like rings on a tree. They signify experience … Make
us unique[1].

Adam: I can see that.

Evelyn: And that's all this is, the idea of you having some surgery. It's
5   an experience …

Adam: I know, it just makes me …

Evelyn: … What, nervous? Of course you should be nervous, why
not? It's something you've never done … But that's the adventure.

Adam: 'It's a far, far better thing I do than I have ever done …'

10 **Evelyn:** Something like that. Is that from a book?

Adam: Yeah, Dickens[2] …

Evelyn: Huh. Well, I don't know about better, but at least different.
(Another quick kiss.) So, are you gonna go check?

Adam: What? … You mean, the rest room?

15 **Evelyn:** Uh-huh.

Adam: Umm … Okay. What if they call my name, though? Seriously …

Evelyn: What if they do?

Adam: *(Smiling)* I smell trouble … Which I may not be able to do
after this.

20 **Evelyn:** Just go …

Adam: *(Standing)* Okay, why not? Then I can show you something …

Evelyn: What?

Adam: Just a little thing I had done. For you.

Evelyn: Wait, what … Show me now.

25 *He looks around, can't wait. He pulls open his pants and lets her
glance inside.*

Adam: Look … A big religious no-no[3]. *(Pulls at his waistband.)* Nice,
huh?

Evelyn: 'Eat.' Lemme guess … You couldn't afford the 'me'.

30 **Adam:** No, you goof! Your initials. Like it?

---

1 unique: *einzigartig*   **2** Dickens: Charles Dickens (1812–1870), British author of
A Tale of Two Cities, from which the quote is taken   **3** no-no (infml): taboo, sth.
that is not allowed

Evelyn: *(touching it)* I do, I like it. And I love the gesture.

Adam: 'Love' is a big word.

Evelyn: I know that. That's why I used it … *(Beat.)* Go check the 'handicapped' stall. I'm suddenly very hungry …

He slips off, out of the waiting room. Evelyn goes back to reading her 5
magazine, when a voice calls out.

Voice: Mr Sorenson. Adam Sorenson, please …

Evelyn looks up, glances toward where Adam has disappeared but says nothing. She smiles.

A LAWN

Phillip and Adam sitting on their jackets between classes, talking.
Adam has a bandage across his nose.

Phillip: I'm serious, it looks good …
Adam: Just shut up … Don't get here late and then make fun of me.
5   **Phillip:** No, you look distinguished[1].
Adam: Phil, I look like a hockey player …
Phillip: Yeah, but a distinguished one.

They chuckle[2].

What'd you do, anyway?
10 **Adam:** … I fell.
Phillip: Come on …
Adam: Seriously, I did …
Phillip: You sound like a battered[3] wife. 'I fell …'
Adam: That's not funny.
15 **Phillip:** Yeah, it is … It's very funny. I mean, it's not that funny that
    wives get beat up, but the fact that you look like one, that I find
    hilarious[4] …
Adam: Well, anyway, that's what happened. I tripped, I fell … No big
    deal.
20 **Phillip:** Sure it wasn't the bathroom door? That's the usual excuse …
Adam: For who?
Phillip: Abused women …
Adam: You're sick.
Phillip: Somewhat, yeah. But I'm nice-looking, which makes up for
25   a lot.
Adam: Not as much as you think …
Phillip: 'Don't hate me because I'm beautiful.'
Adam: I don't … I just hate you.

1 distinguished: having an appearance that makes you look important or that
makes people admire or respect you   **2** chuckle: laugh   **3** battered: bruised
from having been beaten up   **4** hilarious: very funny

Phillip: See, I knew you did, all these years ... *(Beat.)* You really fell?

Adam: Yeah. I tripped on the stairs going into my apartment and caught my face on the ... You know ... The ...

Phillip: No, what?

Adam: Oh, come on! It's not that fascinating ...   5

Phillip: It is, too. It's completely fascinating. So, you don't wanna tell me then, right?

Adam: Tell you what?!

Phillip: What happened to your ...

Adam: I told you. I tripped going up the ... And hit the edge of the ...   10

Phillip: Yeah, it's the 'edge of' that I'm a little hazy on here ...

Adam: Edge of the knob. My door knob.

Phillip: She clocked[1] you one, didn't she?

Adam: Who?

Phillip: 'Who?' The artist, formerly known as Evelyn, or whatever   15
her name is ...

Adam: Are you nuts?

Phillip: Well, I've gotta hand it to her, she certainly made a 'statement' ...

Adam: You are such an idiot ...   20

Phillip: Did she hit you?

Adam: Stop!

Phillip: I don't care if she did, I'm just asking ...

Adam: Yeah, well ... You can be annoying.

Phillip: It's one of my best qualities, actually ...   25

Adam: And there aren't many of them.

Phillip: You really tripped? Truthfully ...

Adam: Yes.

Phillip: ... Huh. Okay.

Adam: Why do you say that? 'Huh.' You don't believe me?   30

Phillip: No, I just ... Nothing.

Adam: What? Don't do that, come on now. What?

---

1 clock sb. (infml): hit sb., esp. on the head

Phillip: It's no big … *(Beat.)* I saw your girlfriend the other day, maybe, what, last Thursday? You weren't in class, and I said to her, I asked her if you were okay, that's all …

Adam: Yeah, so?

5 **Phillip:** And she said 'yes', but you were recovering from an operation or something …

Adam: What?!

Phillip: That's what I said, 'He didn't tell me about anything', and she said it wasn't really an operation *per se*[1], just something you had

10 done. A procedure. And that was it … So I just thought …

Adam: No, it's not …

Phillip: Hey, you don't have to tell me, we're not on intimate terms or anything …

Adam: I hurt it. Really …

15 **Phillip:** Whatever.

Adam: No, not 'whatever', Phil … I did. I hit it and, you know … I banged it pretty bad at home and so I had the doctor look at it. But he didn't … *operate* or anything. The bandage is from that. The door.

20 **Phillip:** After you tripped on the stairs … Yeah, you told me.

Adam: She must've just gotten confused.

Phillip: Maybe. That doesn't seem to happen to her very often, though … She's pretty sharp.

Adam: No, she is … I'm sure it's just the way I explained it. I mean,

25 to her …

Phillip: Right.

Adam: … And where did you see her?

Phillip: Evelyn? I don't know … Starbucks or somewhere. The mall, maybe. Adam: She doesn't drink coffee.

30 **Phillip:** So, it was downtown then, Record City[2], I think … *(Beat.)* What, you worried I'm gonna steal her? Believe me …

Adam: No, God … Don't be so … *(Touches nose.)* Anyway, it's gonna be fine …

1 per se (fml) [pər ˈseɪ]: in itself   **2** Record City: (formerly) shop that sold music

Phillip: Well, that's good to hear.

Adam: Yep.

Phillip: ... So you're okay, though?

Adam: No. I mean, yeah, I'm great ... Absolutely.

Phillip: Then good ... *(Beat.)* And you'd tell me if there was anything 5
seriously wrong?

Adam: ... Of course! Hey, what's up?

Phillip: I mean, we're friends, right? You'd come to me ...

Adam: ... About what? *(Beat.)* Phil, what's ...?

Phillip: Jenny told me. 10

Adam: What?

Adam looks at his friend. For the first time, Phillip seems less than in control.

Phillip: She kissed you.

Adam: Oh. 15

Phillip: She felt shitty, I guess. I could tell for, like, a week that
something was going on and finally she told me about it. How
you guys met and talked about us – why do girls always have to
talk about everything? – and later she leaned over and kissed
you. That's what she told me. 20

Adam: She did ... I mean, she did do that but it was nothing.

Phillip: Hey, it wasn't nothing, she's a good kisser. Hell of a kisser.

Adam: I don't mean 'nothing', but it meant nothing. It didn't hold
meaning for us ... It just happened.

Phillip: Okay. So, you can speak for her, then? 25

Adam: For me ... It didn't for *me*. It was just a ... That's all she said?

Phillip: Don't tell me there's more ...

Adam: No, God, not at all ... I just ..

Phillip: It's alright, I'd been acting weird lately, this whole marriage
idea is just ... freaky ... So, it's my fault. 30

Adam: Right ...

Phillip: I mean, who gets married at *twenty-two* these days? Right? it's not the Middle Ages, for chrissakes[1]... *(Beat.)* I just feel bad ... You know, for her.

Adam: Why?

5 **Phillip:** Kissing you ... That's hideous[2]! It's what those new-age dumbshits would call 'a desperate cry for help' ...

They laugh, catching each other's eye.

Adam: Sorry ...

Phillip: 'S alright. It's better than me having to kiss you ...

10 **Adam:** Good point.

Phillip: No tongue, right?

Adam: Jesus ...

Phillip: I'm just asking ...

Adam: No! Please ...

15 *Phillip looks at his watch.*

Phillip: Well, I got a three-ten[3]. You?

Adam: Nah ... I'm free. Gonna go work out.

Phillip: You and the ... What is going on with the 'metamorphosis'[4] thing here? You're like Frankenstein ...

20 **Adam:** You mean, Frankenstein's monster. Frankenstein was the doctor ...

Phillip: Ahh, don't be such an English Lit prick[5]...

Adam: I am an English Lit prick.

Phillip: I know, but you don't have to sound like one, do you? Doctor,

25 monster, whatever! What's up with that?

Adam: Nothing. It feels good.

Phillip: How much weight have you lost?

Adam: Not that much, maybe ten pounds or ...

---

1 for chrissakes (infml): expression of surprise or anger   **2** hideous: terrible
3 three-ten: class that starts at 3.10 pm   **4** metamorphosis: process in which sb. changes completely into sth. new   **5** prick (sl): offensive word for a stupid or unpleasant man

Phillip: I'd say more like fifteen.

Adam: Yeah, maybe.

Phillip: And the hair thing going, no glasses now ...

Adam: It's just a few little ...

Phillip: Hey, it's the 'new you'. Plus, the nails. Jenny told me that, 5
which is the one that I just cannot believe!

Adam: It's a life change ...

Phillip: Please, don't make me throw up with the Oprah-talk[1],
alright? I'm trying to compliment you here ...

Adam: ... Thanks. 10

Phillip: I used to find blood on our *phone,* okay, so it's not just this
casual thing, quitting ...

Adam: I know. I know that ...

Phillip: Alright, then. *(Beat.)* No, you look good. I can see why she
kissed you ... Hell, I might even kiss you, with a few drinks in me. 15

Adam: *(laughing)* I'll run home and hide the liquor[2] ...

Phillip: Please, I'll help you! *(Beat.)* And nothing else happened,
right, I mean, between you and Jenny?

Adam stops cold. Walked right into a trap.

Adam: ... What? 20

Phillip: I'm just asking.

Adam: Phil ...

Phillip: Not really looking for a speech or anything. Just an answer.
She said 'no', just so you don't think I'm laying a trap[3] here or
whatever ... 25

Adam: I don't.

Phillip: ... Nobody saw you on campus or anything. A ranger out in
the woods. You know, so ...

Adam: ... What's that supposed to mean?

Phillip: I'm just *saying,* I'll believe you, whatever you tell me. I've got 30
no witnesses. So ...

---

1 Oprah-talk (infml): reference to talk show host Oprah Winfrey   **2** liquor
['lɪkər]: strong alcoholic drink   **3** trap: trick

Adam: Nothing happened, Phil. Truthfully.

Phillip: ... That's not what she said.

Adam freezes but doesn't falter.

Adam: That's not true.

5 **Phillip:** You sure?

Adam: Yes.

Phillip: You're right, it's not true. Hey, a man's gotta try ...

Adam: Uh-huh ...

Phillip: Not that I want out of this or anything. I love scuba-diving ...

10 **Adam:** Of course. As we all do ...

Phillip: Exactly. I'm just not sure I wanna share my air tank with the same person the rest of my life ...

Adam says nothing, just smiles. ...

But that's my problem. *(Beat.)* I gotta get to class ...

15 **Adam:** Alright. Take care.

Phillip: Sorry for the, you know, crazy shit.

Adam: It's okay ...

Phillip: ... Don't kiss my girlfriend any more, alright?

Adam: You got it.

20 **Phillip:** See you ... We should do something again one of these days, all of us, I mean ...

Adam: ... Yeah ...

Phillip: If you guys wanna. Let us know. So long, Romeo!

Adam: *(Pulling on a coat)* Knock it off!

25 *Phillip starts off but stops dead. He turns back and studies Adam.*

Phillip: ... Where's your jacket?

Adam: What?

Phillip: Okay, this is too much. The cord jacket, the lumberjacky-looking thing ...

30 **Adam:** I dunno ...

Phillip: And this, umm, Tommy Hilfiger-ish job, where'd you come up with that?

Adam: ... The mall. I bought it.

Phillip: *You* bought some clothes? You, like, went out to the mall on your bike and actually ...

Adam: No, Evelyn drove me. So? What's the big ...?

Phillip: The deal is this ... You've had that frumpy[1]-looking fucker   5
for three years, probably more, and I've never seen you out of
it. *Ever.* Winter, the dead of summer, whatever, you've got that
coat on. And now you're just like, 'Hey, whatever. *(Yawns.)* Yeah,
I bought the ol' stars and stripes here with Evelyn.' That's like a
sailing slicker[2]!   10

Adam: It's their yachtsman line ...

Phillip: I am gonna puke[3] here, I swear to God! I did not just hear
you use the word 'yachtsman' ...

Adam: Hey, she likes it ...

Phillip: Well, isn't that just neat[4]? And peachy keen[5] and whatever   15
other *Little House on the Prairie*[6] shit you wanna spout[7] ... What
I wanna know is, do you like it?

Adam: ... It's okay.

Phillip: Not what I said. I asked, 'Do-you-like-it?'

Adam: It's fine. It's a coat ...   20

Phillip: And lemme ask you ... Did you keep the cord job or did she
make you toss[8] it?

Adam: ... Who cares? This is ... I threw it out, okay? Goodwill[9],
actually.

Phillip: 'Goodwill, actually.'   25

Adam: It's really no big deal ...

Phillip: Dude, don't just say 'no big deal'. I begged you to throw out
the farm coat our freshman year, I mean, you've lost both of us
a lot of dates with that thing on! You've had it since, like, birth,
okay, so do me a little favor and let's not pretend that the jacket   30

1 frumpy: not fashionable   2 sailing-slicker: type of jacket used for sailing
3 puke (sl): vomit   4 neat: good, excellent   5 peachy keen: fine, excellent
6 Little House on the Prairie: popular US TV show (1974–1983) about a 19th
century farmer family in Minnesota   7 spout: (here) say   8 toss sth.: throw sth.
away   9 Goodwill: charity shop that sells second-hand clothes

and the, ahh, weight and the Jon Bon Jovi hair are no big deal. Because when it comes to routine, you used to be like Mister goddamn *Rogers*[1]!

Adam: Phil, it's a fucking jacket, so just lay off[2]. Go to class ...

5 **Phillip:** Uh-huh. Fine ...

Adam: Fine.

Phillip: I just hope next time we pass each other I recognize who the hell you are ...

Adam: Well, if not, you and Evelyn can always head over to Record
10 City and have a chat ...

Phillip: Hey, I wouldn't get too deep into the moral issues during this particular conversation ... Okay, Romeo? I may have a big fucking mouth, but at least I keep it to myself ...

They stare at each other, a nearly visible wall going up between them.
15 *Adam blinks first and walks off.*

Phillip watches him go.

So long, matey!

---

1 Mr. Rogers: reference to the TV show *Mister Rogers' Neighborhood* (1963–2001), whose presenter always wore the same jacket   **2** lay off: stop it

A COFFEE SHOP

Evelyn stands with Jenny at a high table, sipping[1] hot drinks.

Evelyn: ... And you, everything's good?

Jenny: Yeah, you know. Okay.

Evelyn: Huh. Well, that's nice to hear ...

Jenny: You?   5

Evelyn: Oh, you know, pretty great. Just studying, working on my art ...

Jenny: Right, you've got a big thing you're doing, or ... what do you call it?

Evelyn: Thesis project. For my degree ...   10

Jenny: That's terrific.

Evelyn: Yeah. The showing's in a couple weeks ...

Jenny: And it's going well? What is it again?

Evelyn: I never said ...

Jenny: Oh, well, that's why.   15

Evelyn: Right. *(Beat.)* It's this sculpture thingie ...

Jenny: Nice. Mmm, I love the arts.

Evelyn: Really?

Jenny: Yeah, you know, going to movies and stuff. We don't get so many here, we have to drive into the city for any of the newer   20 releases, but I see a lot of videos. Phil watches 'em constantly.

Evelyn: Yeah, and what kind does he like?

Jenny: Oh, a bunch, but more artsy ones than I do ... *Aliens. Blade Runner. Twelve Monkeys*[2]. Is that right, or were there ten of 'em?

Evelyn: No, it was twelve ... A dozen monkeys, I think, all together.   25

Jenny: Anyway, that kind. Sci-fi, but with some meaning, too. And action.

Evelyn: Huh. That's great ... I hate sci-fi. *(Beat.)* And you? What kind do you like, Jenny?

---

1 sip sth.: drink sth. slowly   **2** Alien, Blade Runner, Twelve Monkeys: popular science-fiction movies

Jenny: Umm, any, I don't mind … But I usually like at least some romance in them. That's always nice.

Evelyn studies her for a moment.

Evelyn: Yes … Romance's good. Especially when you least expect it.
5 **Jenny:** Uh-huh …

Jenny looks over, sees that Evelyn is watching her, looks away quickly.

… You know, I was gonna say, I think what you've done with Adam, it's really great.
Evelyn: And what've I done?
10 **Jenny:** You know, just … He's changed.
Evelyn: That's right. *He's* changed.
Jenny: That's what I mean.
Evelyn: He's done the work …
Jenny: Of course, I didn't mean that you …
15 **Evelyn:** I know. I'm just saying, he did it.
Jenny: Right. That's always what they say, though, isn't it?
Evelyn: What? And who are they?
Jenny: You know, like in *Cosmo*[1], when they have those tests, asking what you'd like to change about your guy …
20 **Evelyn:** Ahhh. Now you're gonna get all scientific on me …
Jenny: It's true, though, right? Almost everybody I've gone out with, if you could alter[2] just one thing, or even get them to stop wearing sunglasses up on their head all the time … Then they'd be perfect. It's that sort of deal, isn't it?
25 **Evelyn:** Something like that … Or it could just be that I care about him.
Jenny: Phil's got, like, six of those 'one things', but it's the same idea …
Evelyn: Right. And how is ol' Phil?
Jenny: He's … Phil. Six 'things' away from being amazing …

---

1 Cosmo = Cosmopolitan: a fashion magazine   **2** alter sth.: change sth.

Adam arrives at the table, obviously unprepared to find both women waiting for him. He wears no bandage.

Adam: … Hey, Evelyn. Hi. Jenny, hello.
Evelyn / Jenny: Hi, Adam. Hello.
Adam: I didn't know you guys were … 5
Evelyn: I invited her.
Adam: That's alright, then …
Jenny: I like your new jacket! Phil told me about it …
Adam: Oh, right. Yeah. It's … new.
Jenny: And your nose! God, you okay? 10
Adam: Yep. Course … It was nothing.
Jenny: Falling down's not nothing. *(Studies him.)* Looks okay, though …

An uncomfortable pause. Evelyn looks over at Adam, who clears his throat. 15

Evelyn: You *fell?*
Adam: … Yeah. Anyway …
Evelyn: Anyway, pull up some floor[1]… We got you a cocoa.

He moves warily to them, squeezing in next to Evelyn.

Adam: Thanks. *(To Evelyn)* You don't drink coffee … 20
Evelyn: It's not. It's decaf[2] …
Adam: That's still coffee.
Evelyn: Good point. So I drink coffee, then, I just don't like the caffeine …
Jenny: Me either. 25
Evelyn: Really? You don't like caffeine either, Jenny? Did you know that, too, Adam, that Jenny doesn't like caffeine?
Adam: No. I didn't know that …
Evelyn: See? There's lots you don't know …

They all sip their drinks silently for a moment. 30

---

1 pull up some floor: (here) come and join us   **2** decaf: decaffeinated coffee

Jenny was just saying that she thinks you're great ... I mean, doing great things with yourself.

Adam: Yeah? Thanks, Jenny ...

Jenny: You're welcome. I just ...

5 **Evelyn:** She thinks you're just about perfect now, don't you, Jen?

Jenny: I didn't say that.

Evelyn: So, he's not perfect, then? Obviously his motor control's a bit off, if he fell, but ...

Jenny: I said that you guys are ...

10 **Adam:** Forget about it.

Evelyn: It's true, I'm exaggerating. She said, and I paraphrase, 'He's changed.' but she implied for the better ...

Adam: Well, I agree. I have. And again, thank you.

Jenny: Welcome ...

15 **Evelyn:** I think you've changed, too, Adam. A lot.

Adam: Yeah? How's that?

Evelyn: Well, I mean, it's obvious, all the minor things are pretty obvious, but in subtler[1] ways as well ... You've gotten cuter. And stronger. More confident. And craftier[2] ...

20 **Adam:** 'Craftier', huh?

Evelyn: Apparently so ... That spill[3] you took must've done it.

Jenny: I'm sorry, am I missing something?

Adam: I'm not sure ... *(To Evelyn)* Evelyn, what's up?

Evelyn: Nothing. Not a thing ...

25 **Jenny:** I mean, you knew about him hurting himself, didn't you? *(To Adam)* Phil said you had a big bandage on, so I just figured ...

Evelyn: No, Jenny, I saw it. I'm kidding ...

Jenny: Ahh. I couldn't tell ...

Evelyn: Sometimes it's hard to read me. Know when I'm joking ...

30 **Adam:** Very hard.

Evelyn: It is. But I am ... Joking, I mean. Adam took a bad fall and smashed his nose, but he's okay now... See?

---

1 subtle: not very obvious   **2** crafty: clever at getting what you want, esp. by indirect or dishonest methods   **3** spill (infml): fall

She grabs Adam's face and holds it out for Jenny to look. Adam pulls away, a bit too quickly. ...

It healed well, don't you think?

Jenny: Yes.

Adam: Do you guys wanna salad or something? I'm hungry ...   5

Evelyn: I'm fine. Jenny ... Hungry?

Jenny: I'm okay. *(To Adam)* Your nose looks ... How much weight have you lost?

Adam: Not that much, really.

Evelyn: Twenty-one pounds. *(To Adam)* I peeked, is that alright?   10

He glares[1] at her; Jenny tries to keep up.

Jenny: 'Peeked'?

Evelyn: His journal ... A record of his progress that he's keeping. Twenty-one pounds as of –

Adam: – last Friday. Yeah.   15

Jenny: Really? That's so cool ...

Evelyn: *Cosmo* story in the making, huh?

Jenny: Yep.

Adam: It's good, yeah, I've been keeping at it ...

Evelyn: She knows, Adam, she already said you've 'changed'. And I   20
already agreed. We're past that ...

Adam: Okay, I'm, like, totally lost here ...

Evelyn: You're mentioned in there, too, Jenny.

Jenny: Where?

Evelyn: Adam's journal. I mean, it's a veiled[2] entry but I think it's   25
you ...

Adam: Evelyn ...

Evelyn: I peeked twice. *(To Jonny)* You're right next to someone known as 'cute waitress'.

Jenny: *(Cautiously)* ... Why's that? I mean ... Adam?   30

Adam: You're not. It's ... She's ...

---

1 glare at sb.: look angrily at sb.   **2** veiled: not expressed directly or clearly

Evelyn: Something about a meeting ... And a drive after, in your cute
little V-Dub[1]...

Adam: What're you saying?! Jenny, there's not any ...

Jenny picks up her purse and smiles thinly.

5 **Jenny:** You know what? It's pretty late, I should get ...

Adam: No, don't go ... *(To Evelyn)* Why are you doing this?

Evelyn: I'm just having coffee. Decaf.

Jenny: I need to go.

Evelyn: I just wanna talk about the kiss. Why can't we do that?

10 *The moment hangs. Jenny stops short.*

We should just put it out there ... I'm very open, and I just feel
that ...

Adam: This is inappropriate, okay?

Jenny: *(To Adam)* Did you tell her about the ...?

15 **Evelyn:** No, no, he didn't ... Phillip did. Days ago. We met and he told
me all about it, Jenny. What you told him, anyway. The rest I got
from loverboy's diary ...

Jenny: ... Adam?

Adam: She's making that up ... She's ...

20 **Evelyn:** Am I?

Adam: Yes!

Evelyn: Then set the record straight ...

Adam: I don't wanna do this right now.

Evelyn: Seems a touch late for that.

25 **Jenny:** *(To Evelyn)* Phillip told you about our talk? When? *(Beat.)*
What else did he tell you?

Evelyn: Lots of things ... He's a very chatty guy, when you wind[2] him
up.

Jenny: ... I can't believe it ...

30 **Evelyn:** Then you're never gonna believe the rest of this ...

---

1 V-Dub (infml): Volkswagen car   **2** wind sb. up [waɪnd] (infml): deliberately say
or do sth. in order to annoy sb.

Adam: Evelyn, let's just drop it, okay? If you're angry with me, alright, but this is not …

Evelyn: We're just talking. People need to share more, that's how this stuff happens, this covert[1] stuff, because we hide it …

Jenny: Fine … You want to … Go ahead. Adam wrote something in his journal, obviously, and I told Phil about …

Adam: Jenny, I didn't …

Jenny: What do you wanna hear? We kissed.

Evelyn: No, I knew that … I'm sorry, I've confused you. I meant about my kiss. With Phillip. That's the part I wanted to talk about with you guys … I didn't make that clear?

Jenny: … What?

Adam: That's bullshit …

Evelyn: No, that's getting even. *(Beat.)* Unless you guys have something else to tell me about. Meaning, 'the drive' …

Adam: We didn't go on any …

Jenny: That's not true. You didn't meet Phil …

Evelyn: Ask him.

Jenny: … Or he would've told me … He …

Evelyn: Apparently not.

Jenny: … I'm going. I'm going now, 'Kay?

Evelyn: Fine, then we'll just let that one hang for a bit … The woods, I mean.

Jenny: I'll … see you. Adam, I'm …

Evelyn: *(Calling to her)* You guys are still coming to my showing, right? Phillip said you would!

She is gone. Adam takes a careful sip before speaking. He turns to Evelyn, about to speak, when Jenny returns.

Jenny: *(Directly at Evelyn)* Hey … Look, I don't know why I'm here, I guess I came back to say 'I'm sorry'. Sorry if I've offended[2] you

---

1 covert [ˈkoʊvɜːrt]: secret or hidden   **2** offend sb.: upset sb. with sth. you say or do that is rude or embarrassing

in some way, or done something to make you so indifferent[1] to me, cold or whatever. And I don't mean what's happened, I don't, because I think you've been this way the whole time I've known you. So ... Sorry I'm not an artsy person or cool enough or, you
5   know, I'm not super-smart, sorry about that. But as far as just *being* a person, like, an average-type person ... I'm pretty okay. I am. *(Beat.)* That kinda came out bad, I mean, dumb[2], so I'm just gonna ... Yeah.

She wanders off.

10 **Adam:** ... Okay, that was horrible.
    Evelyn: Oh, I dunno ... I could've told her about the blow job I gave him. *(Beat.)* Kidding ...
    Adam: No, listen, what you did was shitty, and awful and just plain wrong ...
15 **Evelyn:** As opposed to you two sneaking off[3] and making out[4]? Where would that fall on the 'bad behavior' list ...?
    Adam: You had no right to do that.
    Evelyn: True.
    Adam: Make her feel that way ...
20 **Evelyn:** She's got a boyfriend who's shit. Now she knows. Hell, she already knew ...
    Adam: It was still wrong to treat her like that! And me.
    Evelyn: Yeah, let's talk about you ...
    Adam: Go ahead. You seem raring[5] to go.
25 **Evelyn:** You wanna tell me about the rest of your date, or should I ...?
    Adam: She called me, okay, asked if I could get together and talk, you know, about Phil. And them.
    Evelyn: And then you made out. Most natural thing in the world ...

---

1 indifferent to sb./sth.: having or showing no interest in sb./sth.   **2** dumb (AE infml): stupid   **3** sneak off: go away somewhere secretly   **4** make out with sb. (infml): kiss and touch sb. in a sexual way   **5** raring to do sth.: very enthusiastic about starting to do sth.

Adam: It just happened. Look, I was going to say something …

Evelyn: That was Hitler's excuse. Try another one …

Adam: It was a mistake! Okay? I know that …

Evelyn: And how *big* was that mistake? *(Beat.)* I don't care about
what happened. I don't. I just want the truth… I told you about   5
what I did – you think I wanted to kiss that guy? – I only did it
for the effect. But I'm asking you … What else went on? I deserve
to know.

Adam: … Nothing.

Evelyn: You're sticking with that?   10

Adam: Yes.

Evelyn: Even if I tell you I know something else went on.

Adam: How could you? It didn't … And I did not put any 'drive' in my
journal. That was a lie.

Evelyn: No, it was a *bluff.* Because I could sense it … *(Beat.)* And the   15
waitress *was* there …

Adam: I'm telling you the truth. About Jenny, I mean …

Evelyn: I don't believe you.

Adam: … I am!

Evelyn: Then we'll have to leave it at that. Won't we?   20

They stare at one another. She touches her nose.

Oh, and glad to hear about your trip … See you next fall.

Adam: That's a bad joke …

Evelyn: It's a worse lie …

Adam: What was I gonna tell them? Huh?   25

Evelyn: The truth?

Adam: Come on … I took shit about my new jacket! That's all people
say to me any more, 'What's up with you? What's going on?' I
can't exactly spread it around about what I've done …

Evelyn: What? You *fell* …   30

Adam: What're we doing here?

Evelyn: I dunno. You tell me …

Adam: I don't know. I really don't …

Evelyn: Are you tired of me? 'S that it?

Adam: God, no! Are you nuts?!

Evelyn: Then I don't get it … I don't wanna sound ol'-fashioned here, but you're a step away from fucking around on me …

Adam: I would never do that …

5 **Evelyn:** No, you would never do that with *her,* and mostly because she wouldn't. I know the type, she needed a shoulder, well, what the hell, why not a kiss while she's at it, and maybe a quick hand job. Who knows? But she's not gonna screw[1] you and you probably wouldn't be able to get it up, anyway, because he's your

10 best 'bud'. *(Beat.)* But lemme ask you, Adam, if it hadn't been her, if it'd been, oh, say that 'cute waitress' the other night …

Adam looks away; Evelyn doesn't let up…

Didn't think I caught that, did you? The chatty-chat[2] and the extra three bucks on the tip[3].

15 **Adam:** … That was nothing.

Evelyn: It's never anything. Until it's something … *(Beat.)* If it'd been her instead … out on that drive …

Adam: … We-didn't-go-for-a …

Evelyn: … Whatever. But if she'd been there instead, then what? Just

20 ask yourself.

Adam: Jesus, next you're gonna tell me the handkerchief[4] with the strawberries on it is missing …

Evelyn: I don't know that reference.

Adam: Don't worry about it. *(Pleads)* Evelyn, please …

25 *She smiles and begins more gently.*

Evelyn: I just wanna know where we stand … I thought I could trust you.

Adam: You can!

---

1 screw sb. (sl): have sex with sb.   **2** chatty-chat (infml): small talk   **3** tip: *Trinkgeld*   **4** handkerchief: reference to Shakespeare's *Othello,* in which Desdemona loses the handkerchief given to her by Othello, which suggests she is cheating on him

Evelyn: She's your friend's fiancée, Adam. I'm your girlfriend ... Where's the trust in that?

He takes her hand suddenly.

Adam: I'll do anything you want. Okay? I know what I did was wrong, I do, I messed up but I've never done that before. Lied to 5 a person I was going out with ... Shit, I haven't even gone out with someone for the two years before we met! So, tell me what to do and I'll do it ... I just, I just don't wanna lose you.

Evelyn: You're sure ...?

Adam: I am so sure. I love you ... 10

Evelyn: I told you, that's a big word ...

Adam: ... And I'm using it. I do, completely.

Evelyn: Anything I say?

Adam: Anything.

Evelyn: *(without emotion)* Give them up. As friends, both of them. 15 No explanation. Don't see them or speak to them again. Not ever.

Adam: ... Huh?

Evelyn: That's what I want. That's the proof to me about how you feel ...

Adam: Evelyn ... That's ... 20

Evelyn: One should always be careful when asking to be put to a test ...

Adam: ... Jesus Christ ...

Evelyn: So, what's it gonna be, Adam?

Adam: And if I don't ...? 25

Evelyn: Pretty much like these things end. I mean, in life, at least ... If this was a movie, I'd see the light eventually, but no such luck. Final answer?

Adam stares at her for a long moment.

Adam: ... I choose you. 30

She pulls him close and kisses him for a long time.

Evelyn: You choose well, grasshopper ...

AN AUDITORIUM

Phillip standing around, dressed up. Adam enters, holding a glass of punch, tries to go the other way but Phillip stops him.

Phillip: ... Adam, dude, what's up?!

Adam: *(Looking around)* Hey, Phil. How's it going?

5 **Phillip:** You know, okay. So, what, you don't take my calls now?

Adam: No, I've been ... I mean ...

Phillip: 'S okay, I understand. The whole ... thing ...

Adam: Nah, it's just been busy lately. At work and stuff ...

Phillip: Yeah. Whatever.

10 **Adam:** Seriously. *(Beat.)* I need to get a seat ...

Phillip: Hold on, hey ... Where's the fire?

Adam: *(Nervously)* I just wanna ... good spot. *(Beat.)* Where's Jenny?

Phillip: Funny.

Adam: What?

15 **Phillip:** Man, come on ... We broke up. Broke it off, whatever. You knew that.

Adam: What? No, I, when ...?

Phillip: Like, two weeks ago ... Right after ... You know. And I'm sorry about that. I was pissed off, but, I mean ... No call for that

20 'eye for an eye' shit.

Adam: ... It's okay. But you and Jenny're ...? I can't believe that.

Phillip: Believe it. *(Beat.)* She came over one day, after seeing you guys, I guess, and that was it. The ring off, and gone.

Adam: ... I'm sorry.

25 **Phillip:** Listen, no hard feelings[1] ... I was looking to get out, you know that. But once you start making those plans, you know, like picking out *napkins* and shit, it's almost easier to just do the thing! *(Beat.)* You did me a favor, really ... Too young to get hitched[2].

---

1 no hard feelings: used to tell sb. you have been arguing with that you would still like to be friendly with them   **2** get hitched (infml): get married

Adam: I don't know what to say …
Phillip: Don't worry about it. *(Beat.)* You haven't seen her lately, have you? Jenny, I mean …
Adam: No …
Phillip: 'Kay. Anyway, this oughta be good, huh?!   5

They share a light laugh. Jenny walks up the aisle, sees them and goes for a seat.

Adam: Jenny, hi …
Jenny: Oh, Adam … Hello. Hi, Phil.
Phillip: Hey.   10
Adam: I'm sorry about … you guys …
Jenny: *(Glaring at Phil)* Boy, you just can't keep anything to yourself, can you?
Phillip: What?
Jenny: You never change … That's what.   15

She turns and walks off, taking a place in the auditorium.

Adam: What's she …?
Phillip: It's not, like, totally official yet … Ahh, fuck, what're you gonna do?

The lights flicker twice. Adam looks up.   20

Adam: We should find a place to …
Phillip: *(Looking)* There's two over there.
Adam: Umm … Maybe we shouldn't …
Phillip: … Got it. Okay, whatever. Take care, man.

He wanders off. Adam watches him go, then finds a place to sit.   25

Lights go down, theatrical lights up. After a moment, Evelyn (dressed up for her presentation) enters crisply[1] and smiles.

---

1 crisply: in a quick, confident and not very friendly way

Evelyn: Good evening. Thank you for coming out tonight – it's very cold and rainy and I'm sure this is not how most of you would choose to spend your time away from campus ... *On* campus. So, I promise to make this presentation as quick and painless as possible, for most of you at least, and get you back home as swiftly[1] as I can. The accompanying visual portion of this graduate thesis project is currently under review but will hopefully be available in the exhibition gallery down the hall for your perusal[2] next week, so if you don't stay tonight for punch and cookies, umm, please stop by and take a look at your convenience. *(Smiles.)* Okay, that's the boring stuff ...

She turns over a note card.

My task here tonight is to unveil[3] my semester's work, explain it and then smile and shake hands, leaving a few of you to examine it, grade it, etc. In essence, be at your mercy. Which is fine, since I realize I have been my entire academic life – at someone's mercy, that is – which reaches back to when I was five. So be it ... That's the system and one person can't change it ... But perhaps they can make you question that system and your values just a little bit. Thus, my rather, ahh, dramatic presentation at this time. *(Looks over card.)* Blah-blah-blah ...

Evelyn starts to move but steps back into the light, as if she's forgotten something.

Oh, I almost forgot ... And this is fairly personal, probably shouldn't even do it but it really is the capper[4] to my time here at Clarkson, so please indulge[5] me. *(Beat.)* I was given an engagement ring two days ago and I haven't answered the guy yet ... So I wanted to do it this evening. Here goes. This is a beautiful stone and an

---

1 swiftly: quickly   **2** perusal [pəˈruːzl] (fml): examination   **3** unveil sth.: show sth. to the public for the first time   **4** capper (AE): climax, finale   **5** indulge sb.: be generous in allowing sb. to have or do what they like

amazing gesture on your part, for many reasons. By the time I'm through here, I promise that you'll have your answer ...

She shows the ring off to the audience.

My graduate advisor[1] gave me this advice five months ago ... 'Strive[2] to make art, but change the world.' Pretty wise words, 5 I thought, at the time, and so, being a good little student, that's what I set out to do. As you know, every journey begins with a single step – boy, the 'coffee cup slogans[3]' are coming hard and fast tonight – and so I set out to ...

She appears almost nervous, but not quite. She looks at the audience 10
for a moment.

As I looked around my world for something to change, I knew I'd been given a tall order[4]. 'Change the world.' So, I decided to do the next best thing, which was change someone's world. I mean, that's a start, right? One person changes, and then another, and 15 then, well, you get it ... Crude[5] but effective. With that in mind, I present to you this, my newest work. It is a *human* sculpture on which I've worked these past eighteen weeks, and of whom I'm very proud. I cannot legally name him tonight as he hasn't yet signed a waiver[6] for the various items on display in the visual 20 portion, but it's a small college, and a smaller town. *(Laughs.)* So you've got a pretty decent chance at guessing who it is. In fact, I've done all I could to be as visible as possible with him this year – I'm more of a stay-at-home person myself – since I thought that was an important aspect of his unique transformation. The 25 piece itself – him – is untitled since I think, I hope, that it will mean something different to each of you and, frankly, anyone who sees it. His own name, however, is quite apropos[7].

---

1 graduate advisor: tutor   **2** strive: try very hard to achieve sth.   **3** coffee cup slogans: sayings you find printed on coffee cups   **4** be a tall order: be very difficult to do   **5** crude: simple and not very accurate but giving a general idea of sth.   **6** waiver: an official document in which sb. gives up a legal right or claim **7** apropos [ˌæprəˈpoʊ]: (here) not important

She turns over a large photograph from a nearby easel[1]. The face has been blurred[2] out.

I did the MTV thing here on the face … This is a 'before' picture that I had a classmate take of us near the Pizza Hut out by the
5   highway. That was our first official encounter after he asked me out – at his place of work, a big no-no, or so I was told – and it was here that I coaxed[3] him into eating his first vegetarian meal. Well, as vegetarian as a spinach-and-mushroom calzone can be! He also had a salad … Anyway, he told me that, for him, it was
10   a huge deal and it does mark the beginning of my systematic makeover, or 'sculpting', if you will, of my two very pliable[4] materials of choice: the human flesh and the human will. *(Beat.)* I first spotted my chosen base material … It's so funny not to use names! Sorry, but a lawyer actually told me I had to say that,
15   'base material' … on January 9th, the fifth day of winter semester, as I was actively pursuing another set of 'base material'. *(Grins.)* Obviously, my current creation appeared much more right for my work and so I created a scenario that would allow for our eventual, yet seemingly random[5], connection.

20 *She scans the audience.*

Still with me? You're very quiet … Okay. The exhibit itself will give you many first-hand examples of my efforts, some hands-on[6] such as video tapes or sound recordings of our conversations and others more scientific in nature, as in growth charts,
25   X-rays and accompanying data. As you can see from this photo, however, the hair, the glasses, the excessive amount of weight, offered a number of physical areas that made him unique and

---

1 easel: a wooden frame to hold a picture while it is being painted   **2** blur out sth.: make sth. dim or vague so it cannot be recognized   **3** coax sb. into doing sth.: persuade sb. to do sth. by talking to them in a kind and gentle way
4 pliable ['plaɪəbl]: easy to bend without breaking; (here) easy to influence or control   **5** random: not planned   **6** hands-on: doing sth. rather than just talking about it

perfect for this project. A short list of alterations[1] I've induced[2] would include eating better and losing weight – some twenty-five pounds or more – an exercise regimen[3] that included both cardiovascular work and weight training, the purchase of contact lenses, a complete change in hairstyles and significant wardrobe 5 alterations as well. He even tattooed his body for me, without asking ... in a highly questionable place. These are surface items, to be sure, but if I, in fact, tell you that I'm going through with it and marrying the guy, you'd probably all shake my hand and say, 'Wow, how the hell can I do that to my boyfriend?' but this, 10 I'm afraid, was not done out of love or caring or concern ... This was a simple matter of can I instill[4] 'x' amount of change in this creature, using only manipulation as my palette knife[5]? I made sure that nothing was ever forced during our sessions or 'sittings' together – I can't really say they were dates, not on my part, 15 although the illusion of 'dating' was imperative[6] – and that his free will was always at the forefront of each decision. I coaxed, made suggestions, created the illusion of interest and desire, but never said, 'Please do this.' Not once. Any questions yet?

She scans the crowd. 20

Umm ... You may be asking yourselves, 'Well, did she at least tell him?' Of course not, no, I couldn't. Not until tonight, or he really wouldn't be a piece of art. He would be a jilted[7] lover, a spurned[8] fiancé, etc. But he is more than that ... He's my creation. Now, it'll be easy for many of you to condemn my actions as harsh, 25 inhumane or unrealistic as you drive or walk home tonight, but remember this, like so many of you when pursuing your personal

---

1 alteration: change   **2** induce sth.: make sth. happen   **3** regimen ['rɛdʒəmən]: set of rules about food and exercise that you follow in order to be healthy
4 instill sth. into sb.: gradually make sb feel, think or behave in a particular way over a period of time   **5** palette knife: a sculptor's tool to make fine features
6 imperative (fml): sth. that is very important   **7** jilted: being rejected in an unpleasant way by your lover   **8** spurned: being rejected or refused by sb., esp. in a proud way

best in relationships and at work ... I was interested in humanity, yes, but insistent on results above all else. How many here can say that they have never looked at their significant other and / or a business associate and said, 'They're perfect, they're great, except for just *one* thing ...' Well, I too have taken my base materials and honed[1] them into something new, something unique and, in the eyes and standards of society, something arguably[2] improved. But, with the artist's ruthless[3] pursuit of truth and historical disregard[4] for rule and law ... I've gone a step further. I found that, with the right coaxing of my material – yes, 'coaxing' often of a sexual nature, I'll admit – I could hone the inside of my sculpture as well as the surface. I found myself suddenly creating strong moral ambiguity[5] where I could detect only the slightest traces before, often in direct proportion to the amount of external change. This means, as my subject became handsomer and firmer and more confident, his actions became more and more, ahh, *questionable*. Against medical advice, he had work done to his face, cosmetic surgery at age twenty-two, and insisted to those around him that he had merely fallen down. He also started to deceive[6] his friends and myself with greater abandon[7] during this period while showing increased interest in other women. Indeed, he had relations with his best friend's fiancée and continues to harbor[8] details from us about the incident to this day. Moreover, he was willing to give those friends up when asked, walk away from them without any further contact, after said encounter, leading me to an assumption of further wrongdoing with the young woman in question. And, as stated earlier, these universal corrections culminated[9] in an

---

1 hone sth.: make sth. better   **2** arguably: *vertretbar*   **3** ruthless: determined to get what you want and not caring if you hurt other people   **4** disregard: the act of treating sth. as unimportant and not caring about it   **5** ambiguity: *Mehrdeutigkeit*   **6** deceive sb.: make sb. believe sth. that is not true   **7** abandon (n, fml): state without control   **8** harbor sth.: (here) keep sth. hidden   **9** culminate in sth: result in sth.

offer of marriage to me, this coming from a confirmed, albeit[1] young, bachelor. I call this act 'morally questionable' because it seems to be motivated, in my mind at least, as much out of guilt as genuine[2] feelings for me. He has then, as I see it, been utterly and totally refashioned as a person. *(Beat.)* As my grandfather used to say, 'He's a real piece of work ... '

She holds up a large 'after' photo for all to see.

And yet open any fashion magazine, turn on any television program, and the world will tell you ... He's only gotten more interesting, more desirable, more normal. In a word, *better*. He is a living, breathing example of our obsession[3] with the surface of things, the shape of them. *(Beat.)* Now, my work will fade, to be sure. Like chipping[4] marble or crazing[5] paint, it will succumb[6] to a can of Pringles[7], a late morning in bed. To time itself. But for this one glorious moment, it is perfect. As perfect as I made it ... *(To photo)* Not bad, huh? And ladies, he is available. *(To Adam)* This was a startling[8] and unexpected gesture, but obviously, I can't accept ...

She takes off the ring and places it on an easel.

You can examine the stone and setting further when it's placed in the exhibit. *(Beat.)* As for me, I have no regrets or feelings of remorse[9] for my actions, the manufactured emotions ... None of it. I have always stood by the single and simple conceit[10] that I am an artist. Only that. I follow in a long tradition of artists who believe that there is no such concept as religion, or government, community or even family. There is only art. Art that must be created. Whatever the cost. *(Beat.)* With that in mind, I present

---

1 albeit [ɔl'biət] (fml): although   **2** genuine: real, sincere   **3** obsession: person or thing that sb. thinks about too much   **4** chipping: when small pieces of sth. break off   **5** crazing: *abblätternd*   **6** succumb to sth. [sə'kʌm]: give in to sth. you desire   **7** Pringles: (trade name) potato chips   **8** startling: surprising
9 remorse: feeling of being extremely sorry for sth. wrong or bad that you have done   **10** conceit: (here) idea

you with my untitled sculpture and supporting materials tonight. Thank you.

She takes a short bow and steps out of the light.

AN EXHIBITION GALLERY

*Several podiums scattered about with various 'supporting data' on
them. Evelyn standing all alone, punch in one hand, cookie in the
other. After a moment, she takes a nibble. She crosses to a box of
photos and browses. Adam enters and stares at her.*

Adam: ... Not a big 'modern art' crowd, I guess, huh?   5
Evelyn: Hey. *(Beat.)* Glad you stopped by ...
Adam: Yeah, well, I didn't really have anything to do ... Plus, I can't
   show my face in the streets, so it seemed logical.
Evelyn: Look, Adam ...
Adam: Please don't 'Look, Adam' me now, okay, or I might not make   10
   it through this ... *(Beat.)* Just refer to me as 'it' or 'untitled', it'll
   help me keep some perspective[1] here ...

*He wanders over and pours some punch. Stuffs a few cookies in his
pocket. Shoves three in his mouth and chews them down.*

   ... That's gonna shoot some piece of data all to shit, isn't it?   15
Evelyn: Doesn't matter now, do what you want ... You're finished.
Adam: 'You're finished.' Wow. *(Considers.)* Most people just say, 'Hey,
   sorry, can't marry you.' And they say it in private ...
Evelyn: ... Yeah, that might've been a bit too far.
Adam: Oh shit, Evelyn, you are so beyond 'far' that you're in danger   20
   of hitting Uranus. And I mean the planet ...
Evelyn: *(Smiling)* See, you're still funny ...
Adam: Just stop, alright? I was never funny, ever, or good-looking or
   clever. I was nothing until you started dicking around[2] with me.
   I admit it. No-thing. But you know what? I was absolutely fine   25
   with that ...
Evelyn: I know this is a lot for you to take in and everything ...

---

1 perspective: the ability to think about problems and decisions in a reasonable
way   **2** dick around with sb. (sl): causing problems for sb

Adam: Uh-huh … I got a little Gregor Samsa[1] thing going right now, so …

Evelyn: I don't get that …

Adam: Doesn't matter. I do … I get it.

5 *A moment of dead silence.*

Evelyn: … Listen, I know my work relied on not telling you what was going on, but I …

Adam: Here in a 'small town' we just call it lying …

Evelyn: I did lie to you, yes …

10 **Adam:** Yeah, just a little. *(Beat.)* 'I'm a very straight-forward person …'

Evelyn: I had to say that. Sorry.

Adam: You're sorry? Well, that's good … I figured I was gonna have to really work to get that one out of you.

Evelyn: I'm not sorry. I mean, not for what I've done. I just feel bad
15 that you're so upset …

Adam: Oh, I see …

Evelyn: I even thought maybe you could handle it. I did, really … Otherwise I wouldn't have invited you tonight.

Adam: Yeah, just me and two hundred of my closest friends.

20 **Evelyn:** Adam, you don't have any friends. *(Beat.)* You gave up the only ones I've known you to have. Gave 'em up pretty easily …

Adam shivers at this one; she's turned out to be a cool little number[2].

Adam: Geez … Don't hold back at all, please. Call it exactly how you see it.

25 **Evelyn:** I just want to keep it as truthful as possible.

Adam: *(Laughing)* That'll be different …

Evelyn: … You're *so* angry …

1 Gregor Samsa: character in Franz Kafka's novella *Die Verwandlung*   **2** cool little number: (here) sb. with few emotions

Adam: Well, you know, Evelyn, what do you want me to say?! You messed with my life and you put it under fucking glass ... That might make anyone a touch cross[1].

Evelyn: What'd I do wrong? *(Beat.)* Seriously, tell me ...

Adam: Screw you ...   5

Evelyn: You have screwed me. A lot. You wanna watch it? There's a cassette over there somewhere.

Adam: You are seriously twisted up. I mean it ...

Evelyn: Yeah ... What was so bad? I wanna know, tell me ... from your perspective.   10

Adam: I'm not gonna give you a last little thrill. Fuck that.

Evelyn: Listen to your mouth, Adam ... You never used to talk like that.

Adam: You're gonna take credit for that, too, huh?

Evelyn: Nope[2], you picked that up all on your own. Cute guys always   15 have potty[3] mouths. They think it makes 'em cuter ...

Adam: Yeah, well, tell me how 'cute' this one is, then ... Up yours[4], you heartless cunt[5].

Evelyn: So, tell me then. Go ahead, you feel that way about me, you can tell me what I did wrong. *If* I did something wrong ...   20

Adam: You don't see this as wrong?!

Evelyn: I said, you tell me. I wanna know what you think I did ...

He stops for a moment, taking a deep breath. Not really wanting to engage[6].

Adam: You honestly have no concept here ...   25

Evelyn: Just say it ...

Adam: Aww, shit. Look ... I don't have time, okay? I'm not gonna stand here and ...

Evelyn: The exercising? Or was it the new clothes that really bugged you?   30

---

1 cross: quite angry   **2** nope (infml): no   **3** potty: dirty   **4** up yours (sl): expression used to be rude to sb. who has made you angry   **5** cunt (derog sl): insult, esp. for a woman   **6** engage: become involved with and try to understand sth.

Adam: That is not the ...

Evelyn: Everything I did made you a more desirable person, Adam. People began to notice you ... Take interest in you. I watched them ...

5 **Adam:** Well, lucky me. I got to be part of your installation 'thingie'.

Evelyn: You *are* my installation thingie ... *(Beat.)* Look, if you hadn't been here tonight, hadn't heard all this stuff ... wouldn't you still be happy? Waiting at home for me, hoping this went well, wanting to make love ...

10 **Adam:** That's not the point ...

Evelyn: Yes, it is! It's the *total* point. All that stuff we did was real for you, therefore it was real. It wasn't for me, therefore it wasn't. It's all subjective, Adam. Everything.

Adam: Not love. Not cruelty.

15 **Evelyn:** Of course they are ...

Adam: *(Reaching)* I'll tell you something 'real', I should sue your ass.

Evelyn: You could ... I did take that risk.

Adam: That's right, you did, and you're crazy if you think I'm gonna let you put all this shit on display. Our time together. *(Points.)*
20 Those're our video tapes, aren't they? The ... sex ones. They are! You are nuts ...

Evelyn: There's a lot of stuff here. I haven't even put it all out yet ...

Adam: Well, you might as well keep it packed up, then.

Evelyn: You should be proud of it ... most of it ...

25 **Adam:** Just save it, 'kay?

Evelyn: Well, what about your jacket? Where should I put that?

Adam: ... What?

Evelyn: Your old jacket. The one I sprayed my number in, at the museum. *(Beat.)* It was only four bucks at the Goodwill ...

30 **Adam:** ... Why would you buy that?

Evelyn: Just so I'd have it. In case ...

Adam: So, blackmail, too, huh? Ohh, shit ... *(Beat.)* Which page of the 'Scorned Girls' Handbook' is that on?

Evelyn: I dunno, but I bet it's in there ...

35 **Adam:** I do not doubt it.

Evelyn: Just wanted you to know, that's all …

He scans the room, then throws his hands up. He wanders about.

Adam: … Fine.
Evelyn: What?
Adam: It's fine, forget it …   5
Evelyn: What is?
Adam: What the hell … It can't get any worse. You get off[1] on
    showing people my old socks and scuzzy[2] sheets, go for it …
Evelyn: I don't 'get off' on it …
Adam: It means so much to you, have a field day[3] …   10
Evelyn: … Adam, this is my work. *(Beat.)* I'll give back whatever you
    want, soon as I get my grade.
Adam: Whatever …
Evelyn: I will.
Adam: The ring'd be nice. It was my grandma's.   15
Evelyn: I'll take care of it.
Adam: Thanks. Good …
Evelyn: *(Honestly)* … Hard feelings?
Adam: Me? Nah … We had some fun, right?
Evelyn: Yeah.   20
Adam: But, hey, that's subjective.
Evelyn: Exactly.
Adam: Then I had some fun, fell in love and all that … And you got
    yourself a grade and a column inch or two in the college paper.
    Congrats[4]. Seriously … But do me a favor, don't fool yourself and 25
    think that this is 'art'. 'Kay? It's a sick fucking joke, but it is not
    'art'.
Evelyn: Is that right?
Adam: Pretty much, yeah. *(Beat.)* You know, when Picasso took a
    shit, he didn't call it a 'sculpture'. He knew the difference. That's 30

---

1 get off on sth.: be excited by sth., esp. in a sexual way   **2** scuzzy: dirty   **3** have
a field day: be given the opportunity to do sth. that you enjoy, esp. sth. other
people do not approve of   **4** congrats (infml): congratulations

what made him Picasso. And if I'm wrong about that, I mean, if I totally miss the point here and somehow puking up your own little shitty neuroses[1] all over people's laps is actually art, then you oughta at least realize there's a price to it all … You know?
5   Somebody pays for your two minutes on CNN. Someone always pays for people like you. And if you don't get that, if you can't see at least *that* much … Then you're about two inches away from using babies to make lamp shades and calling it 'furniture'. *(Beat.)* Look, I know they call it the 'art scene', but that's not all
10   it should make. A scene. It should be more than that. Anybody can be provocative, or shocking. Stand up in class, or at the mall, wherever, and take a piss[2], paint yourself blue and run naked through a church screaming out the names of people you've slept with. Is that art, or did you just forget to take your Ritalin[3]?
15   There's gotta be a line. For art to exist, there has to be a line out there somewhere. A line between really saying something and just … needing attention. *(Beat.)* … I guess I'm done.

Evelyn: Wow. Okay … So, you're saying I should be a 'better person'. Is that it?

20   **Adam:** That's the nutshell, yeah.

Evelyn: Better like … you?

Adam: No. Just better …

Evelyn: Well, we'll just have to agree to disagree, then, won't we?

Adam: Yes, we will. We will definitely do that. *(Beat.)* Don't forget
25   what Oscar Wilde said …

Evelyn: He always had something to say, didn't he?

Adam: Yeah … 'All art is quite useless.' He said that.

Evelyn: Huh. I thought you were gonna go with 'Insincerity and treachery[4] somehow seem inseparable[5] from the artistic
30   temperament.' That's a good one, too …

---

1 neurosis [nʊˈroʊsəs] (pl. neuroses): strong fear or worry   **2** take a piss (infml): urinate   **3** Ritalin: drug people take who suffer from attention-deficit hyperactivity disorder (ADHD)   **4** treachery [ˈtretʃəri]: behavior that involves not being loyal to sb. who trusts you   **5** inseparable: that cannot be split into two parts

Adam: It is, yeah. Damn, wish I'd said that.

Evelyn: Don't worry about it … Look how he ended up.

Adam: Yep … Alone, penniless and in prison. Everything I wish for you … *(He smiles.)* Tell me, though. One thing.

Evelyn: Yes?   5

Adam: Was any of it true?

Evelyn: What do you mean?

Adam: Not the things we did, or the kind words or whatever … But any of it?

Evelyn: … No. Not really.   10

Adam: I mean about you. The nose-job or Lake Forest or your mother's maiden name? One thing you ever said to me?

Evelyn: My mom's name is Anderson …

Adam: Oh. Are you twenty-five?

Evelyn: Twenty-two. Just … I skipped third grade.   15

Adam: Okay … *(Beat.)* And the scars are …

Evelyn: I made it all up.

Adam: Got it. I got it … Gemini at least?

Evelyn: No, Pisces[1]. Sorry.

Adam: Don't be. Hey, it's … *art.*   20

A moment of silence. They look at each other for a bit.

Evelyn: *(Checking watch)* I should probably get going, I gotta hook up with[2] some guys from my department …

Adam: Alright.

Evelyn: … and I think the Dean wants 'a word' with me, too. *(Ricky*   25
Ricardo voice.) 'I got some 'splaining to do.'

Adam: What's that from?

Evelyn: Nothing. *I Love Lucy*[3].

Adam: Ahh, TV. That other great art form …

Evelyn: Uh-huh. You coming?   30

---

1 Pisces: *(Sternzeichen) Fische*   **2** hook up with sb. (infml): meet sb.   **3** I Love
Lucy: US TV show about Lucy and Ricky Ricardo

Adam: Nah, not yet ... *(Holds up hands.)* Don't worry, I'm not gonna do anything to your stuff. No spray paint. I just ...

Evelyn: I understand. Go ahead.

Adam: Thanks ...

5 **Evelyn:** The door locks if you just close it.

Adam: Great.

Evelyn smiles at him once more, but says nothing. What's to say? She heads for the door but stops.

Evelyn: ... That one time.

10 **Adam:** Huh?

Evelyn: In your bed, one night, when you leaned over and whispered in my ear ... Remember?

Adam: Course. I remember everything about us.

Evelyn: And I whispered back to you, I said ...

15 **Adam:** I remember.

Evelyn: I meant that. I did.

Adam: Yeah?

Evelyn: Yes.

Adam: ... Oh.

20 *She starts to say something else but catches herself. She goes out. Adam stands alone in the quiet room, looking about. He takes a few more cookies, eating them as he wanders around and picks up items from his recent life with Evelyn. He finally stops near the TV/ VCR. Suddenly, he pops in a tape and settles back on the floor. He*
25 *finds the moment he is looking for ... The exchange of whispers. He presses 'play' and watches it. He rewinds and does it again. And again. He scoots[1] over and pulls on his old jacket, huddling[2] there on the ground. He watches the picture intently, but what is being said remains elusive[3]. Unheard. He continues. Silence. Darkness.*

---

1 scoot (infml): hurry   **2** huddle: hold your arms and legs close to your body
because you feel cold   **3** elusive: difficult to define

ADDITIONAL TEXTS

1. NEIL LABUTE INTERVIEWED BY NEV PIERCE

Neil LaBute burst onto the American indie scene with the caustic[1] drama In The Company of Men, *about two blokes who seek revenge against women by seducing and dumping a deaf[2] girl. The acidic* Your Friends & Neighbours *followed, before the sly comedy* Nurse Betty *and period piece[3] / love story* Possession. *With* The Shape of Things *he returns to his roots, adapting his own stage play into an invigorating, provocative exploration of manipulation, sex, art and artifice[4].*
5

The Shape of Things *examines the effect of becoming more superficially appealing. Did you become more desirable once you became professionally successful?*
10

Sure, yes, absolutely. You're embraced in a way. You were the same person, you were always writing the same way, but suddenly there seemed to be a collective turning of the head, toward you. Like anything, too much of a thing can be unbalancing. It's very hard to keep well-adjusted when suddenly there's this wave of interest and desire and all of those things. So yeah, that's difficult.
15

For better or worse, *In The Company of Men* was heavily scrutinised[5] when it came out, and had I allowed myself to soak all of that up and think, 'Oh, this is "Important". What else "Important" do I have to say?', I could probably still be thinking about it now. I'm happy that I went right into something else, and then made another movie, and I haven't really taken time to ever let myself get caught up in what it can mean.
20

You don't sit back thinking, 'I'm Neil LaBute ...'

---

1 caustic: critical in a bitter or sarcastic way   **2** deaf: being unable to hear
3 period piece: a play or movie that is set in a particular period of history
4 artifice (fml): the clever use of tricks to cheat sb.   **5** scrutinise sb./sth.: look at or examine sb./sth. carefully

No. I say, 'I'm Neil LaBute', but I think of it with very little import[1].
I constantly feel the need to, not to prove myself, but just to keep
working. The desire is there to work. I've hung in for a long time
doing work that wasn't getting noticed anywhere outside of the
theatre that it was being done in, so it's nice to have a wider platform
on which to work. I'm just happy to be doing what I always wanted
to do.

When In The Company of Men *came out, a lot of people said you must
be a misogynist2. That was because you were being mean to a woman.
Now you have a woman being mean to a man, so people will label you
as a misogynist again ...*

Yeah, it hasn't helped. If this was my campaign to turn things around,
I went about it badly. Because it's just the other end of the spectrum.
I've had a few of those words levelled[3] at me, but it doesn't faze[4] me
in any noticeable way, because I disagree. I think that I write good
parts for men and women, and I don't look at them in those kind of
political or gender ways. I'm just trying to tell a good story.

Your Friends & Neighbours *was well made but it was like watching
a car accident. It's entertaining, but it's really painful. You think, Do
I want to praise it when it brings out these feelings? You examine the
question in* The Shape of Things: *Is there moral or immoral art? Is that
something you're interested in given your Mormon faith?*

Yes, absolutely. My faith has a definite attitude and thought about
what art should be. That it should be to beautify[5], to enlighten[6] and
all of those things. It doesn't see great value in showing the negative
things, whereas I've always felt you can get to that by showing the

---

1 import (fml): the meaning of sth.   **2** misogynist: a man who hates women
3 level sth against sb: say publicly that sb. is sth.   **4** faze sb. (infml): make sb. feel
confused or shocked   **5** beautify: make sth. more beautiful   **6** enlighten: make
information available about sth.

things, whereas I've always felt you can get to that by showing the negative. So there's been an obvious kind of rift[1] between us, in just mindsets. But I think people are always guided ultimately by that inner thing. They say, 'I've got the compass and I've got to follow that one, whether it's slightly skewed[2] or not. That's the moral compass that I have to go by.' So that's the one that ultimately I'll keep following.

Source: Nev Pierce, website of the BBC

---

1 rift: a serious disagreement between people   **2** skewed: not accurate or correct

2. NOW PLEASE PAY ATTENTION EVERYBODY.
I'M ABOUT TO TELL YOU WHAT ART IS.

What is art? Art is anything an artist calls art. An artist is someone
who makes or does something she or he thinks of as art. Making
pictures can be called graphic art, but it is quite likely to have
nothing to do with art whatsoever. Take the pictures that hang
5 every weekend on the railings of London's Hyde Park, hundreds of
them. No art involved. A graffito[1] on a railway bridge is more likely
to be art, most probably bad art, but art just the same. Most art is
bad, but you don't get the good art without the bad. Our best artists
make stuff they know is bad; the difference is that they destroy it
10 themselves. Tracey Emin[2] didn't wait to be told to destroy the
paintings that earned her an MA[3] at the Royal College of Art. There
are a few dealers around the place who would kill to get their hands
on them; she has made sure they never will. That's the kind of thing
real artists can be expected to do.

15   Art is a part of life, but in order to be art it has to create for itself
a separate zone, what we might call the art space or the art time. A
urinal is not an art object as long as it is carrying out its essential
function. To make it art we detach it from the plumbing, tip it on
its end and set it on a plinth[4]. The beholder then has to entertain a
20 galaxy of new and unfamiliar thoughts about the object, redefining
it and herself in relation to it. The original object, which Marcel
Duchamp[5] called 'Fountain', signing it R Mutt, was rejected by the
Society of Independent Artists at whose New York gallery it was
supposed to be exhibited in 1917 because, they said, it was not art.
25 In 2004, 500 British 'art experts' selected it as 'the most influential
artwork of the 20th century'.

---

1 graffito: singular of graffiti   **2** Tracy Emin (born 1963): British artist   **3** MA
(abbr): (university degree) Master of Arts   **4** plinth: a block of stone on which a
column or statue stands   **5** Marcel Duchamp (1887–1968): French-American
painter and sculptor. His controversial work 'Fountain' (1917) consisted of a
urinal signed R. Mutt.

Human beings have always done art. They have set aside time to carry out activities that did nothing obviously useful. They made images, transformed their bodies with painted marks, told stories, sang and danced. Nowadays, we imagine that these activities were 'timeless'; it would be truer to say that they were 'timeful', sometimes ₅ taking days for preparation, and days for performance. The times and the places they happened in were set aside.

For most of human history, the artist has had no duty to record what things or animals or people actually looked like. The subject of art was more often something that could not be seen, such as the ₁₀ energy of the monsoon, depicted in the rock art of the Australian Kimberley region as the wandjina[1]. In that case the artist was a person apart, a senior lawman who inherited[2] the responsibility of keeping the sacred images fresh. Before he could lay a finger on them he had to travel to the sacred site by a special route and bathe ₁₅ in the clean, cold water of the deep gorges[3]. Sacred is just another name for separate.

Drawing and painting are fun, and most people like doing them, especially if they are considered good at them, but they are not art until they acquire separateness. A recognisable likeness ₂₀ of a celebrity will be artless, unless it acquires its own position in relation to all the other images of that celebrity and celebrity itself. Andy Warhol refined the image of Marilyn Monroe till it was almost insubstantial, a hieroglyph in place of a likeness, with neither age nor identity nor expression. It may seem the diametric[4] opposite of ₂₅ the most famous portraits of history, but it isn't. The portraits that survive have outlived their subjects and taken on a life the subjects could never claim. Those pictures exist in their own versions of the wandjina / Warhol zone.

---

1 wandjina: cloud and rain spirits in the Australian Aboriginal mythology
2 inherit sth. from sb.: receive sth., e.g. money, property, from sb. when they die
3 gorge: canyon   **4** diametric: complete

Studying art for A-level is really tough because of the inherent[1] contradiction between being trained to reach a standard and finding out how to be spontaneous. The value the examiners demand is creativity, but creativity cannot be taught. Lady Gaga has said: 'Once
5   you learn to think about art, you can teach yourself.' She might as well have said: 'Once you learn to think about art, you can only learn from yourself.' You can be taught to draw like somebody else, but you can only learn to draw like yourself from yourself. Supposing drawing is your kind of art, and supposing you are really serious.

10   The kids who get up at midnight and head out to a derelict[2] wall to begin working on a graffito are working within a demanding tradition that requires the sequence of execution to have been worked out in detail in advance, before any mark can be made. They can make no money out of what they do. There are no prizes
15   for them. They could go to jail. There is no truer example of the sacredness of the art enterprise than this.

Source: Germaine Greer, The Guardian, *6 March 2011*

1 inherent: that is the basic part of sth.   **2** derelict: run-down

3. IS COSMETIC SURGERY THE NEW ACCEPTABLE FACE OF WOMANHOOD?

Here is a confession: at 44 years of age, I have the face and body I deserve. My upper arms are fleshy and fulsome[1], bearing no resemblance to the sleek[2] undulations[3] of gym-honed[4] muscle I paraded in my twenties. [...] My complexion reflects more than three decades of suffering from acne. In short, my face is, well, my 5
face. It tells an honest story of a life lived. My life.

And there's the rub[5]. There shouldn't be anything unusual in that but, increasingly, I'm aware that I'm in the minority when I mix in certain circles. Arriving at some social events or work appointments, I find unfamiliar faces looking back at me from 10
people whom I know well. These are women who appear one day with startled[6] expressions, unable to smile warmly as they used to, their skin taught, waxy and translucent – like glassine paper[7].

Having 'work' done is the new norm, you see, and I am conscious that, while I am content to look my age and confidently declare 15
myself an intervention-free zone, I frequently stand out from the scalpel-ed, Botox-ed crowd as the one 'who doesn't'. This is not some self-indulgent[8] plea for validation but an observation that the Stepford-style[9] masses are becoming the acceptable face of womanhood. [...] 20

'I think people chase compliments and once we start getting those, we want more,' says Dr Frances Prenna Jones, a London-based cosmetic doctor who counts a plethora[10] of magazine beauty editors and celebrities [...] as clients. 'Most women come to me and their concern is that they look "tired". They might not feel 25

---

1 fulsome: *üppig*   **2** sleek: smooth   **3** undulation: curvy shape   **4** gym-honed: trained and shaped in a gym   **5** there's the rub: here's the problem or difficulty   **6** startled: surprised, alarmed   **7** glassine paper: *Transparentpapier*   **8** self-indulgent: selfish   **9** Stepford-style: reference to *The Stepford Wives* (1975), an American science-fiction thriller about a small town where the wives have been replaced by robots that fulfill their husbands' wishes   **10** plethora (fml): an amount that is greater than is needed or can be used

tired on the inside but they want the outside to reflect how they feel. Increasingly, I am using vitamin injections to give a natural, fresh-faced radiant[1] appearance. Volume replacement[2] (using hyaluronic acid[3]) is popular, too, but you need to take into account
5 the naturally changing proportions of the face. If what you see is markedly different to what you expect, then it jars[4].'

TV presenter and journalist Anne Robinson, herself no stranger to the cosmetic surgeon's scalpel, says 'anything that allows women to feel better about themselves is worth it'. And clearly, many of her
10 compatriots are with her on that one. According to the most recent figures from the British Association of Aesthetic Plastic Surgeons, which represents one in three cosmetic surgeons in the UK, 50,122 surgical procedures were performed here in 2013, excluding walk-in[5] treatments such as Botox. [...]

15 If we simply accept these 'ideals' as purported[6] by the media, and go to such great lengths and take risks to conform to them, what are the implications? With society's compulsion[7] to share selfies, often distorted using photo-manipulation software and always curated[8] to display our 'best self' – whatever that is – is this tsunami of
20 cosmetic surgery just the next phase in a vanity-obsessed culture? [...]

Polly Vernon, author of *Hot Feminist,* believes that women have the right to choose and take ownership of their appearance. 'But I would say that at this point in time women are succumbing[9] to
25 cosmetic surgery because they feel a pressure to,' she says. 'When we inject our faces with stuff, that doesn't come from the same place as putting on a colourful lipstick. We are navigating a new world, where we are much more conscious of our image, and we must own it and delight in it, rather than do things because of social pressure.

---

1 radiant: showing great happiness or health   **2** volume replacement: giving the face a rounder look by injecting fillers which remove wrinkles   **3** hyaluronic acid: *Hyaluronsäure*   **4** jar (v): look strange   **5** walk-in: without an appointment   **6** purport sth: claim to be sth., when this may not be true   **7** compulsion (fml): strong pressure to do sth   **8** curate sth.: carefully select sth.   **9** succumb to sth: not be able to fight against sth.

Appearance should be an extension of who you are, not about trying to be someone you think society wants you to be.' [...]

'I do hear women talking about the pressure to look good,' says Susan Harmsworth, founder and chairman of beauty company ESPA, who recently celebrated her 70th birthday and proudly claims she is regularly mistaken for a woman in her 50s – without having done anything other than led a healthy lifestyle with regular facial massages and skincare regime. 'I know lots of high-profile, successful, intelligent women who have had work done, especially in the City, in banking and law, because they feel they need to look a certain way in the workplace, but once you start messing with your face, you start to look strange.'

With a seven-year-old daughter, I fear for the expectations of the next generation of women, who are likely to have little respect for the glorious beauty of age and the natural lines that come with wisdom.

Psychologist Ros Taylor, author of *Confidence at Work*, says: 'The availability and accessibility of cosmetic procedures, the lack of stigma[1] about having work done and the rise in women's disposable income has meant the gateway is clear for this to become normalised. And it is only going to increase. I feel a little like King Canute[2] seeing this wave coming and being unable to stop it.

'Women are always blaming themselves for their lack of success, or not being tall enough, slim enough, beautiful enough. We constantly compare and contrast ourselves to other women, and although we are mostly fine as we are, we constantly desire to be different. The psychological impact of seeing someone different in the mirror can't be underestimated.'

It is this broader impact of cosmetic intervention that Dr Mark Henley, of the British Association of Plastic Reconstructive and Aesthetic Surgeons,, says led to the organisation's 'Think Over

---

1 stigma: feeling of disapproval that people have about particular illnesses or ways of behaving   **2** King Canute: English king (995–1035) who showed that waves cannot be stopped no matter how powerful the ruler

Before You Make Over' campaign to educate the public on safe cosmetic surgery. 'One of the things we have to do is give people a reality check on what are normal human behaviours and values, and what is social pressure.

5   'They may have perfectly reasonable reasons for wanting surgery, but we mustn't enthusiastically accelerate[1] them towards the theatre[2] as a commercial commodity[3]. We must get it right in terms of counselling, preparation and information about potential risk and benefits. We need to ensure the patient has a good mental

10 insight and understanding of the limitations of proposed surgery, and they have to be in the right frame of mind: no divorce or deaths, which make them emotionally unstable and vulnerable.

'If I think someone is addicted to the high of procedures, I want them to see a psychologist or their general practitioner. No one ever

15 said Margaret Thatcher or the Queen should have a facelift. If in doubt, don't. That's a really good starting point.'

Source: Karen Kay, The Guardian, *28 June 2015*

---

1 accelerate sth.: make sth. happen faster or earlier than expected   **2** theatre: *Operationssaal*   **3** commodity: product

THE AUTHOR

Neil LaBute is one of the most prolific contemporary dramatists. He has been dubbed 'a chronicler of cruelty' for his controversial and provocative plays, in which the characters often reveal an evil or immoral side.

Neil LaBute was born in Detroit, Michigan, in 1963. His parents, a truck driver and a housewife, moved to Spokane, Washington, where he grew up. He discovered his ambition to write while working as a projectionist in a movie theatre.

© Aaron Eckhart

Studying theatre on a scholarship by the Brigham Young University in Provo, Utah, he teamed up with Aaron Eckhart, who went on to become a Hollywood actor and starred in several of LaBute's plays and movies, to perform his first major play *In the Company of Men* (1993). At university he met his wife, Lisa, with whom he had two children before separating in 2010, and converted to Mormonism.

LaBute left university with degrees in Theater and Film. He attended the University of Kansas and received his Masters degree in Theater and Film. He also graduated from New York University (Master of Fine Arts in dramatic writing) and was the recipient of a literary fellowship to study at the Royal Court Theatre, London.

LaBute has written and directed more than 20 plays which have premiered both on Broadway and in London's West End. He has successfully adapted some of his plays into movies (the best-known examples are *In the Company of Men* starring Aaron Eckhart and *The Shape of Things* with Paul Rudd and Rachel Weisz) and produced, directed and written screenplays for several movies. In 2013 he received an Arts and Letters Award by the American Academy of Arts and Letters. Lately, LaBute has also turned his attention to TV work. He has contributed work to acclaimed series such as *Billions, Hell on Wheels and Van Helsing*. He has also written and produced several short films and written short stories.

The Shape of Things, directed by LaBute himself, first premiered in London at the Almeida Theatre in 2001 and was met with critical acclaim. It was awarded the *Drama Desk Award for Outstanding Play* in 2001. In 2003, LaBute adapted the play into a movie with the same cast as in the London theatre production, which won him the *Storyteller Award* at the Taos Talking Picture Festival. *The Shape of Things* was performed in 14 theatres in German-speaking countries in the 2002 season and continues to be staged in theaters all over the world.